PRACTICAL ENDGAME
PLAY

PRACTICAL ENDGAME PLAY

NEIL McDONALD

CADOGAN
chess
LONDON, NEW YORK

First published 1996 by Cadogan Books plc, London House, Parkgate Road, London SW11 4NQ.

Distributed in North America by Simon & Schuster, Paramount Publishing, 200 Old Tappan Road, Old Tappan, New Jersey 07675, USA.

British Library Cataloguing in Publication Data
A CIP catalogue record for this book is available from the British Library

ISBN 1 85744 176 1

Typeset by ChessSetter

Printed in Great Britain by BPC Wheatons Ltd, Exeter

Contents

Introduction

The great World Champion Capablanca once gave the following advice to chess players:

"The game might be divided into three parts: opening, middlegame and endgame...Whether you are a strong or weak player, you should try to be of equal strength in the three parts." *My Chess Career*, Dover 1966.

For a long time I couldn't understand this advice. Certainly, I thought, it would be good to be equally strong in all phases of the game, but I would rather be good in one phase, say the middlegame, than be equally weak in all phases!

However, bitter experience eventually taught me what Capablanca meant.

There is nothing more frustrating than to play a nice attack in the middlegame, win a pawn, follow the prescribed recipe of simplifying to an endgame, and then...agree a draw!

Yet many players who are stuffed full of opening theory and middlegame tactics are helpless in the endgame. Some years ago at a tournament in France, I was completely outplayed by a young French player, and adjourned the exchange down in a simple position. During the adjournment, I happened to speak to a couple of other French players who asked me about my game. I told them I was losing and then, full of admiration for my opponent, I predicted that he would soon become a Master or Grandmaster. Unexpectedly, this statement caused laughter. "Don't worry!" came the eventual reply "If there is a way to draw, he'll find it!" It seems that my opponent's play had already established a reputation among French players, although perhaps not of the best sort...

The game resumed and immediately my adversary began hesitating over his moves. Again and again he missed simple wins until finally he "found the way to draw". I was pleased at having survived but also felt sorry for my opponent: it was as if a substitute player had taken over from the confident, precise player I had faced in the first session.

Even if you are a strong middlegame player it will only occasionally be possible to strike a knockout blow which avoids the endgame. The rest of the time you will have to try to exploit any advantage gained in the endgame, and what can be more demoralising than to know that you had a winning advantage but couldn't clinch it?

Therefore, Capablanca was right. You should work on all departments of your game and make them equally strong. If you are strong in one or two phases of the game, you have to raise your understanding of the rest.

This brings us to the purpose of our book. Its aim is to help the reader improve his knowledge of what is for many players their weakest area: the endgame.

Almost all of the examples are taken from modern, top class grandmaster games. It seems to me that most books on the endgame, including recent ones, have unjustly neglected the games of the modern masters. Although I am a great admirer of the endgame virtuosity of Capablanca, Rubinstein and the other old masters, they have no monopoly on endgame technique.

The examples are grouped under seven headings, but most of them demonstrate more than one important endgame principle. This is only natural since strategy is built upon many themes, not just one. Furthermore, in most of the examples the analysis of the game begins some moves before the critical phase is reached. This is to allow the reader some perspective on how play developed, or perhaps to illustrate some interesting tactics or strategy. Therefore, the reader shouldn't be surprised if the discussion of a minor piece endgame begins in a more complicated setting with queens and rooks still on the board.

In some cases a large number of tactical variations have been given to support the general descriptions of the games. If the reader finds an example particularly interesting (or strongly disagrees with the assessment of a position!) he should study these variations. However, it is by no means necessary to plough through all the tactical analysis for improvement. A great deal can be learnt just through following the strategic reasoning in each game.

I hope the reader enjoys this survey of the endgame and is helped to improve his play even slightly. Then the book will have served its purpose.

Neil McDonald
July 1996

1 Pawn Endgames

Since pawns are the soul of chess, this is an appropriate place to begin our analysis of the endgame.

In the first part of the chapter, various strategic themes are discussed. Of these, it is essential that the reader grasps the concepts of zugzwang, the opposition and the outside passed pawn. These motifs are common to all types of endgame, not just pawn endgames, and so must be fully understood. Otherwise phrases used later in the book, such as "zugzwang breaks the opposition", will appear to be gobbledegook!

In the second part there are illustrative games. While writing this section, I was reminded of a conversation I once had with a draughts (chequers) expert, who suddenly declared that draughts was a more difficult game than chess! Before I could respond to this heresy, he asked me sharply:

"How many moves ahead do you calculate?"

"I'm not sure, maybe four or five moves" I replied. He shook his head sadly, and my chess playing instinct told me I had fallen for a trap.

"Four or five moves! well, I have to calculate 30 moves ahead!"

All my subsequent attempts to persuade him that four or five moves with queens and rooks were more difficult to calculate than 30 moves with counters proved fruitless.

Now I think perhaps he was right! It all depends on how you measure "difficulty". Pawn endgames are the nearest that chess gets to draughts. As in draughts, variations are sometimes very long but there is always a final solution to be found: it is within the capacity of the human brain to calculate a position to a win, loss or dead draw. In contrast, a typical middlegame or even endgame is so complicated that there is no chance to analyse it out. Then the player has to switch to a strategic assessment such as "here I should put my rook on the seventh rank". The sheer complexity of chess often makes it less "difficult" than draughts in terms of the demands it places on the player's ability to calculate. Of course, in defence of our game we can argue that there is more to chess than calculation, but it is time to look at some pawn endgames.

The opposition: King and pawn against king

In this diagram the two kings are facing each other. This means that the player to move has to

give way with his king. Therefore White to move has to play ♔d4 or ♔f4, when ♔f5 or ♔d5 will let the black king advance. Black to move first would have to play ...♔f6 or ...♔d6, when White is free to advance ♔d5 or ♔f5. Thus the player who is not to move actually has the initiative, since his opponent can only play a weakening move and then his own king will be the first to go forwards across the rank that divides them. Alternatively, if the player not to move prefers to prevent his opponent's king advancing at all, this can also be achieved. Thus after **1 ♔d4** Black can play **1...♔d6 2 ♔c4 ♔c6 3 ♔b4 ♔b6** etc. keeping the two kings facing each other. Then the white king can never break into Black's half of the board. With Black to move first, White can meet **1...♔f6** by **2 ♔f4** when **2...♔e6 3 ♔e4** or **2...♔g6 3 ♔g4** prevents the black king ever advancing.

Whoever is **not** to move first in such a position is said "to have the opposition". The question of the opposition is almost always crucial, indeed often decisive, in pawn endgames. Here is perhaps the most important diagram in the whole book.

White to move can only draw against best play, while Black to move loses. This is due to the opposition principle. We can verify this by analysis.

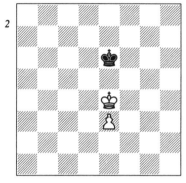

First, Black to move: **1...♔d6** (1...♔f6 leads to equivalent play, starting 2 ♔d5) **2 ♔f5 ♔e7 3 ♔e5 ♔d7 4 ♔f6 ♔e8** (if 4...♔d6 5 e4) **5 ♔e6 ♔d8 6 e4 ♔e8 7 e5 ♔d8 8 ♔f7 ♔d7 9 e6+ ♔d8 10 e7+ ♔d7 11 e8♕+** and wins.

What have we seen? On every rank the opposition compelled Black's king to give way to the white king, until finally it was driven back to the back rank. Then the white pawn advanced, and when it was appropriate, the white king gained control of the queening square and shepherded the pawn home.

Now let's see what happens when it is White's move in this above diagram.

1 ♔d4 ♚d6 2 ♔e4 ♚e6 3 ♔f4 ♚f6. The white king finds its forward path blocked. The squares in front of it are always inaccessible. What if he tries going round the edge? (from the diagram) **1 ♔d4 ♚d6 2 ♔c4 ♚e5** and if now **3 ♔c5 ♚e4** wins the pawn.

So the white king has to stay fairly close to his pawn and is unable to push the black king out of the way. But what if White tries advancing his pawn? **1 ♔d4 ♚d6 2 e4 ♚e6 3 e5 ♚e7! 4 ♔d5 ♚d7 5 e6+ ♚e7 6 ♔e5 ♚e8! 7 ♔d6 ♚d8 8 e7+** (there is no way to make progress) **8...♚e8 9 ♚e6** stalemate.

Now imagine that if at move six in the last variation Black had been unaware of the necessity of keeping the opposition and played 6...♚d8?. Then after 7 ♔d6 the two kings are face to face again, and horror of horrors for Black, it is his move! After 7...♚e8 8 e7 ♚f7 (White to move could only stalemate with 9 ♚e6 here) 9 ♔d7 the pawn queens. Such is the power of the opposition. As a rule of thumb, when defending such a position it is generally best for Black to avoid diagonal moves backwards. He should follow the lead of the white king, that is, he should retreat directly backwards in front of the pawn if the white king is directly or diagonally behind the pawn, or go sideways to

face the white king when it has moved to the side of the pawn.

Several further observations should be made on this endgame. Firstly, when White is to move he can sometimes gain the opposition (i.e. give Black the move when the kings are face to face) by playing a pawn move.

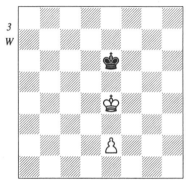

3
W

Here we have the above endgame but with the pawn on e2 rather than e3. This means that White to move can play **1 e3!** gaining the opposition. Then **1...♚d6 2 ♔f5** wins as in the first note to diagram 2 above.

The same possibility is present with the white king on e5, the pawn on e3 and the black king on e7. 1 e4! wins.

This gives us a general principle viz.: if there is an intervening square between the white pawn and the white king then White to move always wins this type of endgame.

An exception to the above analysis occurs if the white king is on the sixth rank. Then he wins in all cases, even without the opposition or a pawn move. Thus with a king on e6, a pawn on e5 and the black king on e8, White wins with 1 ♔d6 ♔d8 2 e6 ♔e8 3 e7 ♔f7 4 ♔d7. Why should this be the case, when with White to move, Black drew in the notes to diagram 2 above, despite having his king driven to the back rank? The difference is that here White still has the opposition-gaining move e6! available to him at the critical moment. In the draw of diagram 2, he had to "spend" e6 earlier to help force Black's king back.

Finally, it should be mentioned that the rook's pawn is an exceptional case. If the defending king succeeds in getting in front of the pawn then there are no winning chances. The king can never be evicted, only stalemated. The edge of the board negates the advantage of the opposition. For example, with White's king on g6 and a pawn on h7, and Black's king on h8, which is of course stalemate, White would win if Black had to play ♔i7...

It is important that the reader understands the winning and drawing methods above. This is because it is a fundamental endgame that frequently has a bearing on how other, more complicated endgames, must be handled. So to reinforce the above here are two examples from the author's own games.

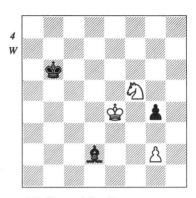

McDonald – Beaumont
London 1995

White played
   55 ♘e3
when if 55...g3? 56 ♘c4+ wins a piece. If Black exchanges pieces then he has a lost pawn endgame after 55...♗xe3 56 ♔xe3 ♔c6 57 ♔f4 ♔d5 58 ♔xg4 ♔e6 59 ♔g5 ♔f7 60 g3 (or 60 ♔h6) 60...♔g7 61 g4, with the standard position where White has the opposition. So in the game Black gave up the g-pawn and brought his king over.

55	...	♔c6
56	♘xg4	♔d6
57	♔f5	♔e7
58	♔g6	♔f8
59	♘f6	♗c1
60	g4	♗d2!

As long as Black controls the g5-square White can't make any progress.

61	♘d5	♗c1
62	♔f5	♔f7
63	♘f4	

The only try to achieve the g5 advance.

63 ...   &xf4!

Now the pawn endgame is a draw after 64 &xf4 &f6 65 g5+ &g6 etc. So a draw was agreed.

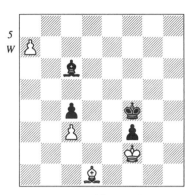

McDonald – Laine
Hastings 1994/5

Play went:

67 &a4!   &a8

If 67...&d5 68 &b5 and 69 &xc4.

68 &b5   &e5

The c-pawn cannot be saved, so Black has to bring his king over to the queenside to stop White advancing his c-pawn.

69 &xc4   &d6
70 &f7   &c7
71 &h5   &b6
72 &xf3   &xa7

Black has succeeded in eliminating White's dangerous a-pawn, but the pawn endgame is now lost.

73 &xa8   &xa8
74 &e3   &b7
75 &d4   &c6
76 &c4

If it were now White to move the game would be a draw, but of course White has the opposition and the black king must give way.

76 ...   &d6
77 &b5   &c7
78 &c5   &d7
79 &b6   &c8
80 &c6   &d8
81 c4

and Black resigned.

The finish would be 81...&c8 82 c5 &d8 when we know from the examples above that even with White to move it is winning with the king on the sixth rank in front of the pawn. Thus if Black could play 82..."Pass" then White wins with 83 &b6 &b8 84 c6 &c8 (if 84...&a8, then 85 c7? stalemates, so 85 &c7! intending 86 &d8 and only then 87 c7 would be called for) 85 c7 &d7 86 &b7 and the pawn queens.

Now imagine that Black had answered 67 &a4 with 67...&b7 (rather than 67...&a8). Then after 68 &b5 &e5 69 &xc4 &d6 70 &f7 &c7 71 &h5 &b6 72 &xf3 &xa7 73 &xb7 &xb7 we have the game position but with the black king on b7 rather than a8. This difference means it is a draw: 74 &e3 &c6 75 &d4 &d6! and Black has the opposition with a standard draw after 76 &c4 &c6 or 76 c4 &c6 77 c5 &c7 78 &d5 &d7! (maintaining the opposition) 79 c6+ &c7 80 &c5 &c8 81 &d6 &d8! 82 c7+ &c8 83 &c6 stalemate.

So 67...&b7 draws, but 67...&a8 loses! That is how accurate you must be in simple endgames.

Zugzwang

Zugzwang is German for "move compulsion" but is now universally accepted as an English expression (at least in chess circles!). We have already seen examples of zugzwang in our discussion of the opposition above. In diagram 2, the two kings are facing each other, and whoever has the move is at a grave disadvantage: White to move only draws, Black to move loses. This is what zugzwang means: you are said to be "in zugzwang" if it is your turn to move and any move you can make is harmful to your own position.

Here is a good example of a fatal zugzwang.

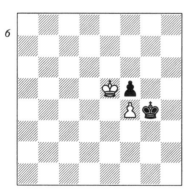

This is mutual zugzwang. Whoever has the move must give up the defence of his pawn, thereby losing the game. The following diagram shows a practical implementation of this idea.

White threatens to march his passed pawn through, so Black

I. Sokolov – Dautov
Ter Apel 1995

decided to sacrifice his knight and then try to achieve a draw by eliminating all the kingside pawns, apparently a good idea.

55	...	♘c4+
56	♔b5	♘xa5
57	♔xa5	♔c5!
58	♗f3	♔d4
59	♔b5	♔e3
60	♔c4	♔f2
61	♔d4	h5
62	♔e4	♔g3

It appears that Black's scheme has been successful, since he is ready to play 63...g4 64 hxg4 hxg4 when the bishop has to move, allowing ...♔xg2 with a draw. But he has reckoned without zugzwang!

63 ♔e5!   g4

If 63...♔h4 64 ♔f5 is another zugzwang. That is why White played his king to e5 last move rather than f5, since he wanted it to be Black to move after 64 ♔f5.

64 hxg4   hxg4

65 ♔e4!

and Black resigned since he is in the zugzwang of diagram 6 after 65...gxf3 66 gxf3.

Here is a well known zugzwang position.

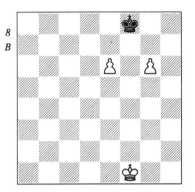

White can promote a pawn without using his king. At the moment Black's king holds up the advance of the passed pawns, but it is his move and wherever he goes he has to allow one of the pawns to queen, for example 1...♔e8 2 g7 or 1...♔g7 2 e7. White to play can just wait with his king.

There are, of course, more complicated zugzwang positions but for the time being it is sufficient for the reader to be aware of the concept.

Creating a passed pawn

This is a common theme which will be examined in detail in chapter 5.

Here we will be satisfied with just one very famous example.

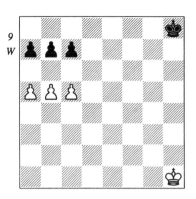

White to move plays **1 b6!** and after both **1...axb6 2 c6! bxc6 3 a6** and **1...cxb6 2 a6! bxa6 3 c6** he has created an unstoppable passed pawn.

Shutting in the opponent's king

It may seem that **1...♔b2** wins for Black. Not so. After **2 ♔d2 ♔xa2 3 ♔c2** Black has broken in and gained some booty, but then finds he can't get out. He has the choice between a draw by repetition (3...♔a1 4 ♔c1 ♔a2 5 ♔c2) or a draw by stalemate (3...♔a1 4 ♔c1 a2 5 ♔c2.)

If there were other pieces or pawns on the board then Black would have winning chances as he could try to free his king. On the other hand he would have losing chances in some situations. Imagine if in the above diagram there were white pawns on g2 and h2 and a black pawn on g7. Then after 1...♔b2 2 ♔d2 ♔xa2 3 ♔c2 ♔a1 4 h4 a2? Black loses: 5 h5 (not 5 g4 g5! 6 hxg5 stalemate) 5...g5 (5...g6 6 h6!) 6 h6 g4 7 h7 g3 8 h8(♕ or ♗) mate: White has just beaten the stalemate! Black also loses after 4...g5 5 h5!, but 4...g6! holds the draw, e.g. 5 g3 a2 6 g4 g5 and White can only stalemate with 7 h5 or 7 hxg5.

Of course, this shutting in procedure is mostly associated with the rook's pawn.

Shutting out the opponent's king

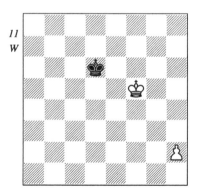

If White pushes his pawn then Black draws easily: 1 h4 ♔e7 2 h5 ♔f7 3 h6 ♔g8 etc. with a standard draw: the black king can never be driven away. Or the white king can become shut in after 1 h4 ♔e7 2 ♔g6 ♔f8 3 ♔h7 ♔f7 etc. White has to block the approach of the black king: **1 ♔f6!** does the trick, for example **1...♔d7 2 ♔f7** (also 2 h4 ♔e8 3 ♔g7 wins) **2...♔d6 3 h4 ♔e5 4 h5 ♔f5 5 h6 ♔g5 6 h7** and wins.

White's king could be said to "shoulder out" his adversary. In Diagram 7 above we saw Rustem Dautov use this technique. Black wanted to move his king over to the kingside, but rather than the direct 57...♔e5 he manoeuvred in such a way as to obstruct, at least for the moment, the approach of White's king. This theme is closely linked to the opposition precept described above (see under Diagram 1).

The feint to defend a pawn

This theme was best exemplified in a study by Réti:

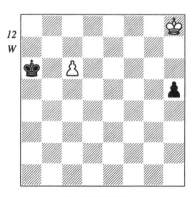

R. Réti 1922

White looks completely lost, as his king is too far away to either defend his c-pawn against capture after 1...♔b6 or to prevent the h-pawn queening after 1...h4. However, White can make a feint to defend his c-pawn which wins him time to head off the black pawn.

After **1 ♔g7! h4 2 ♔f6 ♔b6** (if 2...h3, then 3 ♔e7 h2 4 c7 ♔b7 5 ♔d7 draws) **3 ♔e5!** White's king has chosen a path to the centre that intersects with two separate designs. If now **3...♔xc6**, then **4 ♔f4** wins the h-pawn. **3...h3 4 ♔d6 h2 5 c7 ♔b7 6 ♔d7** is also drawing, when both pawns queen. A beautiful study, but is it of any practical value? The following dispels any doubts.

cannot be stopped. I was hoping that my opponent hadn't seen Réti's study, but he instantly replied

    66 ♔b7!

and a draw was agreed. After 66...♔xa5 (or the a-pawn queens) 67 ♔c6 the white king gets back in time to stop the h-pawn.

Two pawns against one on the same side

This is normally a win. It is usually only necessary to make sure that a pair of pawns aren't exchanged in such a way as to give a drawn king and pawn versus king endgame.

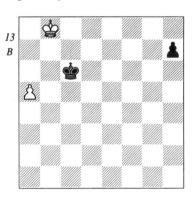

Wynarczyk – McDonald
Whitby 1992

    65 ...   ♔b5

This move appears to win, because 66...♔xa5 is threatened and after 66 ♔c7 h5 the passed pawn

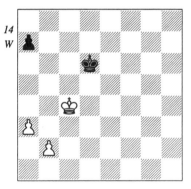

Lautier – Piket
Dortmund 1995

First of all White ties down the black king to the a7-pawn. This takes two moves.

    53 ♔b5   ♔c7
    54 ♔a6   ♔b8

Then he moves up his a-pawn.

55 a4	♔a8
56 a5	♔b8

Now comes the tricky part. Lautier wants to play b6 when the black king is on a8, so that White will have the opposition. If he plays 57 b4? ♔a8 58 b5 ♔b8 59 b6 axb6 60 axb6 ♔a8 Black has the opposition and it is a draw after 61 b7+ ♔b8 62 ♔b6.

So White has to get the timing right.

57 b3!	♔a8
58 b4	♔b8
59 b5	♔a8
60 b6	

and Black resigned.

After 60...axb6 (60...♔b8 61 b7) 61 axb6 ♔b8 62 b7 wins.

Outside passed pawns and decoy pawns

It is usually a great advantage in a pawn endgame to have an outside passed pawn or the pawn majority on the opposite wing to the main body of pawns. This is because an outside passed pawn can be used to deflect the enemy king away from the defence of his main mass of pawns, which in his absence can be gobbled up by one's own king.

White played **40 e4!** Black dare not answer **40...♕xe4+** because after **41 ♕f3+ ♕xf3+ 42 ♔xf3** the king and pawn endgame is easily won for White because of the outside pawn, e.g. **42...♔e6 43 a4** (even simpler is 43 g4)

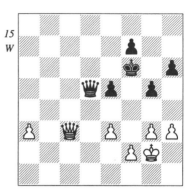

Bareev – Karpov
Belgrade 1996

43...♔d5 44 a5 f5 45 a6 ♔c6 46 g4 fxg4+ 47 hxg4 ♔b6 48 ♔e4 ♔xa6 49 ♔xe5 ♔b6 50 ♔f6 ♔c6 51 ♔g6 and Black loses both his kingside pawns.

In the game, Karpov tried 40...♕a2 but resigned after 41 ♕c5 ♔g6 42 ♕d6+ ♔h7 43 ♕d5!

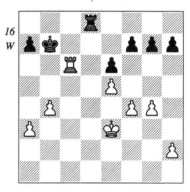

Hawksworth – McDonald
Edinburgh 1985

Here the author found out about pawn majorities the hard

way. White gave back his extra pawn to force a winning pawn ending: **37 罝d6! 罝xd6** (37...罝c8 38 罝d7+ is intolerable) **38 exd6 含c6 39 含d4 含xd6 40 h4 h6 41 a4 g6** (this makes it very easy for White by allowing him to fix the black kingside pawns. However, there was no longer any hope, e.g. 41...f6 42 b5 g5 43 hxg5 hxg5 44 fxg5 fxg5 45 a5 and the black king will be deflected to the queenside after b6, when 含e5 will win his kingside pawns.) **42 g5 hxg5 43 hxg5** and Black resigned. After b5, a5 and b6 the road to f6 will become clear.

More complex examples on this theme will be found in Chapter 5.

Illustrative games

The following games demonstrate the principles expounded in the section above. For the sake of completeness a detailed analysis has been included to justify the general strategic verdicts expressed. The reader may find this difficult at first, but don't worry: in the games the players themselves made some terrible errors. The important thing is to grasp some of the recurring themes, not to calculate ten moves ahead.

In Adams-Lutz it may appear at first glance that White's queenside pawn majority gives him the better chances. However, Black's king is more active than his counterpart, he has a space advantage

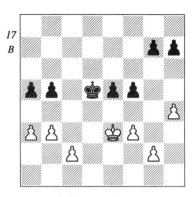

Adams – Lutz
Wijk aan Zee 1995

(his territory consists of four ranks, White has three and there is a "no man's land" along the white fourth rank) and, crucially, there is an important weakness on White's c3 square. Black is in fact winning!

The game came to an abrupt end after

| **30** ... | **a4** |
| **31 h5** | **b4!** |

and White resigned, because next move a black pawn will appear on a3, either by ...a3 or by ...bxa3, and the white king will be unable to prevent it queening. This neatly illustrates the theme of breakthrough (see page 15 above). The analysis that follows is rather more complicated!

Lutz studied this endgame in *Informator 62*, and was critical of the play of both White and Black. Instead of 30...a4, which gave White the chance to save himself, he points out that Black should

have played **30...h5!** This would
rule out any White counterplay
with g4 (why this is important
will be explained below). White is
helpless, e.g. **31 ♔d3 a4 32 bxa4**
(32 b4 e4+ and the black king will
penetrate to b2 via c4 and c3, winning the a3-pawn. Here also the
black e-pawn will be used to dis-
tract the white king if it tries to
set up a blockade) **32...bxa4 33
♔c3 e4 34 fxe4+ fxe4 35 ♔d2
♔c4 36 ♔e3 ♔c3 37 ♔xe4 ♔xc2**
followed by capturing on a3 and
queening the a-pawn. We can see
the importance of Black's e-pawn
in this sequence. The black king
can always force its way past its
counterpart and capture White's
queenside pawns because the forward advance of the e-pawn compels the white king to give way.
Using the pawn as a decoy is a
very important theme.

In the game, Black failed to
take the precaution of sealing
the kingside. After **30...a4** White
should play **31 bxa4** (ruling out
the ...b4 trick) **31...bxa4 32 g4!**

Now the game can finish in two
distinct ways.

a) If **32...fxg4 33 fxg4 ♔c4 34
♔e4**, then while Black is capturing on c2 and a3 and queening
his a-pawn, the white king eats
through the black kingside, and
establishes a drawn queen versus
pawns endgame.

Here is a plausible endgame
that could arise. Black to play
would win easily if there were no

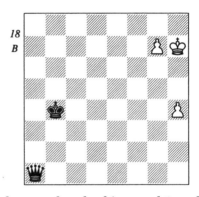

h-pawn by checking on h1 and
eventually forcing the white king
in front of the g-pawn (see our
section on essential knowledge).
However, there is an h-pawn and
it provides vital shelter for the
white king. After 1...♕b1+ 2 ♔h8
♕b2 3 h5 a possible draw is
3...♕f6 4 ♔h7 ♕f7 5 h6 or even 5
♔h6 (threat 6 g8♕! ♕xg8 stalemate) 5...♕g8 6 ♔g6 ♔c5 7 h6
♔d6 8 h7 ♕e6+ 9 ♔g5 etc.

b) **32...g6 33 gxf5 gxf5 34
♔d3!** (keeping the black king out
of c4) **34...h5** and now White just
scrapes a draw with **35 c3! ♔c5
36 c4**. If it were now White's
move he would be in zugzwang
and lose after 37 ♔c3 e4. That is
why White played 35 c3 rather
than 35 c4. With Black to move it
is a draw (although only just):
36...e4+ (Black has no way to
lose a move, e.g. 36...♔b6 37 ♔d2
♔c6 38 ♔c2 ♔c5 39 ♔d3 etc. and
it is still Black to move. In this sequence White always has to be
ready to answer ...♔c5 with ♔d3.
Thus he would lose after 36...♔b6

37 ♔d2 ♔c6 38 ♔d3? ♔c5 since Black has successfully given him the move: White must play 39 ♔c3 allowing 39...e4.) **37 fxe4 fxe4+ 38 ♔xe4 ♔xc4 39 ♔e3!** (going after the h5-pawn is too slow here) **39...♔b3 40 ♔d3 ♔xa3 41 ♔c3**. Then the following position could easily be reached.

Black's only winning chance is to attempt to queen the h5-pawn. So imagine that Black marches his king over to the kingside and captures the h4-pawn. White's king must first deal with the pawn on a3 and only then follow the enemy monarch towards the kingside. The reader can verify that White succeeds in capturing the a3-pawn and reaching f1 with his king while Black is playing ...♔xh4 and ...♔g3. Hence, Black lacks one tempo to cut off the approach of the white king with ...♔g2, when the h-pawn is unstoppable. So Black has the choice between allowing the white king to h1 or burying his own king in

front of the h-pawn, with a total draw in either case (see sections pages 15 and 16 above).

In this variation we see why it was so important for White to reduce the number of kingside pawns with 32 g4! If White still had a pawn on g2 and Black a pawn on g7 then the arrival of the black king on the kingside would have been decisive.

After seeing the incredible length and subtlety of these variations (which are based on Lutz's excellent commentary) it seems somewhat harsh to append question marks to the blunders that both sides made in the game. If we are looking for the guiding thread of a principle to trace our way through the maze of lines that prove 30...h5! for Black and 31 bxa4 bxa4 32 g4! for White to be the best moves, perhaps we should talk about "restraining the opponent's counterplay" or "gaining space", but even then I would bet on a computer against Karpov in such a position!

In our next example the complexities of a pawn endgame also proved too much for the human brain.

1 ...	b4?
2 g4	fxg4
3 fxg4	h6

Because the b-pawn is so vulnerable White would easily win the race to queen a pawn after 3...♔e5 4 g5! ♔f5 5 ♔xd4 ♔xg5 6 ♔c4 ♔g4 7 ♔xb4 ♔h3 8 a4 etc.

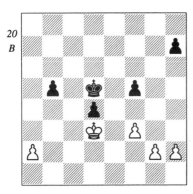

Dreev – Stohl
Brno 1994

4 h4   ♔e5

5 h5! and Black resigned.

Black is in zugzwang (see page 14). If he plays 5...♔d5, then 6 g5! will queen, or if 5...♔f4, then 6 ♔xd4 ♔xg4 7 ♔c4 ♔xh5 8 ♔xb4 ♔g4 9 a4 and White's pawn is much the faster. Note that if White had played the obvious 5 g5? then 5...hxg5 6 hxg5 ♔f5 7 ♔xd4 ♔xg5 and Black's king can rush back to blockade the a-pawn, reaching a8 in time to achieve a standard draw. Dreev chose 5 h5 to entice the black king as far away as possible from his a-pawn.

Stohl analysed the diagram position in *Informator 61* and found the saving defence. The following comments are based on his conclusions.

Black should begin with the pawn advance **1...h5!** restraining White's kingside pawns by preventing g4. Curiously, this is exactly the same plan that Black should have employed in Adams-Lutz above.

a) If White now tries to force g4 with **2 h3?** he even loses as a result of zugzwang after **2...h4! 3 a3** (3 f4 b4) **3...f4** and White has run out of pawn moves and is therefore compelled to retreat his king, when 4...♔f4 will win comfortably.

b) So White has to prepare g4 more slowly with **2 g3 b4!** (only thus; 2...♔c5 3 a3! ♔d5 4 h3 ♔e5 5 g4 hxg4 6 hxg4 fxg4 7 fxg4 ♔d5 8 g5 ♔e5 9 g6 ♔f6 10 ♔xd4 ♔xg6 11 ♔c5 wins because the white king captures the b-pawn and then cuts of the approach of the black king with ♔c6 and ♔c7 or ♔b7 when appropriate, thereby allowing the a-pawn to run through, e.g. 11...♔f7 12 ♔xb5 ♔e7 13 ♔c6! ♔d8 14 ♔b7! ♔d7 15 a4 ♔d6 16 a5 – this is according to the section on page 16) **3 h3 ♔c5 4 g4 hxg4 5 hxg4 fxg4 6 fxg4 ♔d5 7 g5 ♔e5 8 ♔c4** (here we see a vital difference from the variation given in the previous bracket above; if White tries 8 g6 ♔f6 9 ♔xd4 ♔xg6 10 ♔c4 the white king is on c4, not c5, and therefore unable to "shoulder out" his adversary after 10...♔f7 11 ♔xb4 ♔e7, so the black king will block the pawn) **8...♔f5 9 ♔xb4 ♔xg5 10 a4** (10 ♔c4 ♔f6! moves into the square of the a-pawn) **10...♔f4! 11 a5 d3** and the black king will shepherd the d-pawn to its queening square with a draw.

c) Finally, Stohl considers **2 a3** when Black has to play **2...f4!** Now Black threatens 3...h4! when he will win by zugzwang. Therefore White must play 3 g4 or 3 g3.

c1) If **3 g4** then **3...hxg4 4 fxg4 f3!** draws.

Here both sides have mutually supporting passed pawns, but different types: White's are linked, Black's divided. The result is an impasse. Neither black pawn can advance without being captured, yet equally White cannot capture either without allowing the other to queen.

Play could go **5 g5 ♔e5 6 h4 ♔f5 7 ♔d2 ♔g6** and since 8 ♔e1? d3 wins for Black, all White can do is move his king to d3 and back again to d2. Meanwhile, all Black can do is keep his king blocking White's passed pawns. So a draw is inevitable.

c2) **3 g3 fxg3** (Stohl also examines 3...♔e5!? which is OK for Black) **4 hxg3 ♔e5 5 ♔e2 ♔d5 6 ♔d2!** (setting a trap) **6...♔e6!** (and not falling for it! Black would be in zugzwang after 6...♔e5 7 ♔d3 ♔d5 8 f4. His king would have to move to c5, away from White's f-pawn, and White would win by 8...♔c5 9 f5 ♔d5 10 f6 ♔e6 11 ♔xd4 ♔xf6 12 ♔c5; Black has to arrange it so that ♔d3 can always be answered by ...♔e5) **7 ♔d3 ♔e5**. Chances are equal, for example **8 f4+ ♔d5 9 f5** (much less effective with the black king on d5 rather than c5) **9...♔e5 10**

f6 ♔xf6 11 ♔xd4 ♔g5. Black is a tempo up on the line above, and this means that after 12 ♔c5? ♔g4 13 ♔xb5 ♔xg3 14 a4 h4 15 a5 h3 16 a6 h2 17 a7 h1♕, Black, not White, queens first and therefore wins! So White would have to avoid this line with **12 ♔e3**, and acquiesce to a draw.

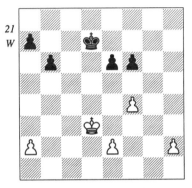

Kramnik – Lautier
Belgrade 1995

In this example the outside passed pawn gives White a decisive advantage. Kramnik's winning plan is to use his h-pawn to deflect Black's king away from the defence of his queenside pawns. Then after capturing both the queenside pawns with his king, White can queen the a-pawn.

Black can only draw if he can sacrifice his two queenside pawns for White's one queenside pawn, and then liquidate all the kingside pawns in the absence of the white king. This, however, proves impossible against precise play.

29 ♔c4

Threatening to win at once with 30 ♔b5 and 31 ♔a6.

29 ...   a6

He has to shut out the white king but in doing so he weakens the queenside pawns.

30 f5!

A classic breakthrough. If now 30...exf5 then 31 ♔d5 f4 32 h4 ♔e7 33 ♔c6 and wins (Kramnik).

30 ...   ♔d6
31 fxe6   ♔xe6
32 ♔d4   ♔f5

Black gives way with his king, but as Kramnik shows in *Informator 65* he has no saving move, e.g. 32...f5 33 e4! fxe4 34 ♔xe4 b5 35 ♔d4 ♔d6 36 h4 and if Black goes after the h-pawn White carries out his standard plan of capturing the black queenside pawns and queening the a-pawn.

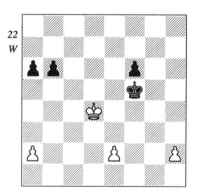

33 ♔d5   ♔f4
34 ♔e6   f5
35 e3+   ♔g4

If 35...♔xe3 then 36 ♔xf5 and 37 h4 wins. Now there begins a

very artistic finish in which the h-pawn advances from h2 to h7 in five consecutive moves.

36 h3+!

Capturing this pawn always allows ♔xf5 when the e-pawn promotes by force.

36 ...   ♔g5
37 h4+   ♔g6
38 h5+   ♔g5
39 h6   ♔g6
40 h7!

At last the pawns wish for self-sacrifice can no longer be ignored.

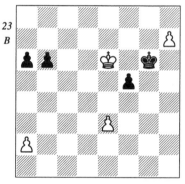

40 ...   ♔xh7
41 ♔xf5   ♔g7
42 ♔e6

and Black resigned. If 42...b5 then 43 ♔d5 and White captures the queenside pawns, but not 43 ♔d7 a5 44 e4? (44 ♔c6 and 45 ♔b5 still wins) 44...b4 45 e5 a4 and both sides queen.

It is important to be aware of possible pawn endgames that can arise from more complicated positions. Whether a pawn endgame is winning or drawing can have a crucial influence on the moves selected, as the following example shows.

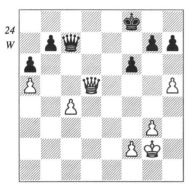

McDonald – Csom
Budapest 1996

The white queen is powerfully placed in the above diagram. I countered the threat to exchange it by ensuring that the pawn endgame would be winning.

    36 f4!   **♕c6**
    37 ♔f3   **♔e7**

Black loses the pawn endgame after 37...♕xd5+ since his b7-pawn is weak and White's d-pawn is strong, for example, 38 cxd5 ♔e7 39 ♔e4 ♔d6 40 ♔d4 ♔d7 41 ♔c5 ♔c7 42 d6+ ♔d7 43 ♔d5 and zugzwang forces the black king to give way.

    38 ♔e4   **♕e6+**
    39 ♔d4

This time the pawn endgame is drawn after 39 ♕xe6+ ♔xe6 as White has no passed pawn: the c4-pawn is as weak as b7.

    39 ...   **♕d6**

    40 ♔e4   **♕e6+**
    41 ♔d4   **♕d6**
    42 f5   **♕b8**

Here 42...♕d7? 43 ♕xd7+ ♔xd7 44 ♔d5 puts Black in zugzwang. A possible finish would be 44...♔c7 45 h6! (45 ♔c5 also wins) 45...gxh6 46 ♔e6 b6 47 axb6+ ♔xb6 48 ♔d6! a5 49 c5+ ♔b5 50 c6 and White wins the race to queen.

The best try was 42...♕xg3, but after 43 ♕xb7+ White has winning chances.

    43 ♕e6+   **♔f8**
    44 ♔d5

Now the threat of 44 ♕d6+, simplifying to a winning pawn endgame, forces Black to bury his queen.

    44 ...   **♕a8**
    45 c5

and Black resigned as 45...b5+ 46 c6 leaves him without defence against the passed pawn.

In our final example, both players ignored or misassessed the complexities of a possible pawn endgame.

Play continued **34...♖c2? 35 c6? h5 36 ♖c8 ♔f5 37 c7 ♔g5 38 ♔f1** and a draw was agreed, since White can make no progress e.g. 38...♖c1+ 39 ♔e2 ♖c2+ 40 ♔d1 ♖c4 41 ♔d2 ♖c5 etc. and the white king has no entry points .

In the game both players were convinced that the passed c-pawn was White's only chance for advantage. They overlooked his possible winning chances in a king and pawn endgame.

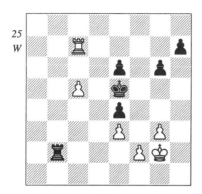

Bates – McDonald
Sevenoaks 1996

After **35 Rxh7! Rxc5 36 Rf7!** the black king is cut off from the kingside, so White is ready to play ♔h3, ♔g4 and ♔g5, winning the g6-pawn. During the game both players thought Black could draw easily by entering a pawn endgame after **36...♔d6 37 ♔h3 Rf5 38 Rxf5**, but it is by no means simple. For example, if 38...exf5 39 ♔h4 ♔e6 40 ♔g5 ♔f7 41 g4! White wins a pawn and the game

after both 41...fxg4 42 ♔xg4 intending 43 ♔f4 and 41...♔e6 42 ♔xg6 fxg4 43 ♔g5 etc.

However, according to the following analysis by John Nunn, it seems that Black can draw with **38...gxf5!** when

a) **39 ♔h4** and now:

a1) **39...♔e5?** 40 ♔g5 ♔d6 (or 40...♔d5 41 ♔f4, followed by 42 g4, wins) **41 ♔f6 ♔d5 42 ♔f7!** (not 42 ♔e7 ♔e5 43 ♔e8 ♔d6 44 ♔d8? e5! drawing) **42...♔d6 43 ♔e8! ♔e5 44 ♔e7 ♔d5 45 ♔d7 ♔e5 46 ♔c6**, penetrating to e5, and then g3-g4 wins.

a2) **39...♔d5 40 ♔g5 ♔c5** answering ♔f4 by ...♔d5 and ♔f6 by ...♔d6, holding the draw.

b) **39 g4** and now Black can draw by either 39...♔e7 40 ♔h4 ♔f6 41 ♔h5 fxg4 42 ♔xg4 e5! and White cannot win, alternatively 39...fxg4+ 40 ♔xg4 ♔d6 (but not 40...♔d5? 41 ♔f4) 41 ♔g5 ♔c5 and Black maintains the opposition.

2 Essential Knowledge

In the later stages of the endgame, the reader has to ask himself questions such as "if I exchange off the queenside pawns can I win with rook and one pawn against rook?" or "if I swap rooks and let my opponent queen first does my pawn on the seventh rank guarantee a draw?"

It is often by no means easy to answer such questions. That is why it is important to memorise a large stock of standard endgames. For example, in answer to the second question above, theory says that an f-pawn, c-pawn, a-pawn or h-pawn on the seventh rank, supported by the king with the enemy king distant, should draw the game (see diagram 35 below). Think how much calculation such knowledge saves! Furthermore, if the player didn't know such a drawing possibility existed, he might not even consider it and instead try a losing variation.

Moreover, think how embarrassing it would be if you had an extra queen but then blundered into this drawing scenario! How would you explain it to your teammates? Read this chapter and you will never have to.

We shall begin with the difficult subject of rook and pawn against rook, which has been analysed for over 500 years.

Two classical rook and pawn endgames

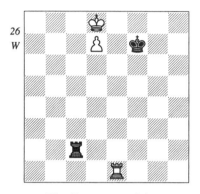

26
W

The Lucena position

This is probably the most famous and instructive example in rook and pawn theory. It was first recorded way back in 1497 by the Spanish author Lucena. Incidentally, his book (a mixture of love poetry and chess problems) has claim to fame as being the first printed work to contain chess analysis. What a deluge of books there have been on chess (and love) since then!

White has an extra pawn one square from queening, but how is he to win? The white king is trapped in front of the pawn, and the attempt to escape with 1 ♖f1+ ♚g7 2 ♚e7 allows Black to check him until he is forced back in front of the pawn: 2...♖e2+ 3 ♚d6

♖d2+ 4 ♔c6 ♖c2+ 5 ♔b5 ♖d2 (or simply 5...♖b2+) 6 ♔c6 ♖c2+ 7 ♔b7 ♖d2 (again, he could carry on checking with 7...♖b2+) 8 ♔c8 ♖c2+ 9 ♔d8 and we reach the diagram position again. So is it a draw?

White's first move was correct: **1 ♖f1+**, driving the black king away and so making an escape route for White's own king, but after **1...♔g7** (obviously 1...♔e6 2 ♔e8 wins) White has to use his rook to shield his king from the checks of the black rook. This cannot be done with 2 ♖e1 (intending 3 ♔e7) because Black's king returns to f7.

The correct method is **2 ♖f4!** which is sometimes known as "building a bridge" (according to Nimzowitsch White's king needs something to sleep under). White wants to move his king out and then block the checks from the black rook by using his own rook on the fourth rank. Therefore, the game could end **2...♖c1** (there is nothing better) **3 ♔e7 ♖e1+ 4 ♔d6 ♖d1+ 5 ♔e6 ♖e1+ 6 ♔d5 ♖d1+ 7 ♖d4!** and White wins. Note that the rook had to be employed on the fourth rank and no other. For example, if White had played 2 ♖f5 then 2...♔g6 would obstruct his plan. Or if 2 ♖f3 then 2...♖c1 3 ♔e7 ♖e1+ 4 ♔d6 ♖d1+ 5 ♔c6 ♖c1+ 6 ♔d5 ♖d1+ and White is unable to prepare the blocking move without losing his pawn (he would have nothing better to do

than move his king back to d8 and then play ♖f4!).

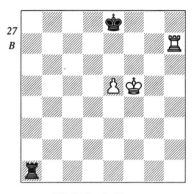

27
B

Philidor's Draw

This is named after the great French player and musical composer François Philidor, who published his famous work "L'analyse du jeu des Echecs" in 1749.

White's winning chances depend on the further advance of his king, either to e6 or f6. So Black plays **1...♖a6!** cutting off the approach of the white king. Then after **2 e6**, the white king no longer has access to the e6-square, but there is a threat of 3 ♔f6 winning. So Black plays **2...♖a1!**, answering **3 ♔f6** with **3...♖f1+**. White's king has no shelter from Black's checks, and even if he did there would be no way to progress. Note that White cannot build a bridge as he did in the Lucena position, because all plausible pawn endgames are a draw, for example 3 ♖h4 ♖f1+ 4 ♔f4 ♖xf4+ (or simply 4...♖e1) 5 ♔xf4 ♔e7 and we know from chapter one that White cannot win.

This technique can be summed up "move the rook to the third, stay there until the pawn advances, then go behind and start checking". Here follows a practical example of this drawing technique.

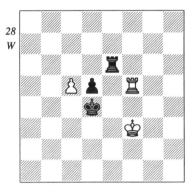

28
W

David – Hebden
Linares Zonal 1996

White gave up his pawn with **42 c6!** to deflect Black's rook and so allow the king to cross the e-file. There followed **42...♖xc6 43 ♔e2 ♔e4 44 ♖h5 ♖c2+ 45 ♔d1 ♖f2 46 ♖h4+ ♔d3 47 ♖h3+ ♔c4 48 ♖h4+ d4 49 ♖h3!** (the key move; now the players could have abandoned the game as a draw) **49...♖b2 50 ♖a3 ♖h2 51 ♖f3** (White patiently waits for Black to advance his pawn) **51...♔d5 52 ♖g3 ♔e4 53 ♖a3 ♖h1+ 54 ♔d2 ♖h2+ 55 ♔d1 d3** (at last!) **56 ♖a8!** and a draw was finally agreed.

But what happens if it is White to move in Diagram 27? He can take the chance to play

1 ♔f6!

Now that the white king has penetrated the third rank it makes no sense to play 1...♖a6+?. Indeed, this move loses after 2 e6, as there is no time to move behind and start checking: 2...♖a1 3 ♖h8 is mate. Black would have nothing better than 2...♔d8, when 3 ♖h8+ ♔c7 4 ♔f7 ♖a1 5 e7 wins – after 5...♖f1+ White can play as in the Lucena position above with 6 ♔e8 followed by building a bridge, alternatively he could exploit the favourable position of his rook, which guards the queening square, by simply approaching the enemy rook: 6 ♔g6 ♖g1+ 7 ♔f5 ♖f1+ 8 ♔g4 etc., reaching g2 when the checks will run out and ...♖e1 can be answered by queening.

So Black needs an alternative drawing method. It is best to play

1 ... ♖e1!

putting the rook behind the pawn straight away. If now 2 e6 ♖f1+ draws as above, and if 2 ♔e6 ♔f8 (or 2...♔d8) draws. The following exemplifies this.

In the next position the author managed to save a draw by remembering the analysis above.

74 ♖h2 (but of course not 74 ♔xe6?? ♖a6+) **74...♔e8 75 ♖d2** (75 ♔xe6 ♖a6+ is our easy draw above, so White avoids the immediate capture) **75...♖e1!** (75...♖a6

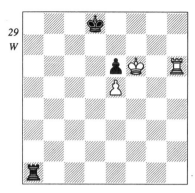

Belkhodja – McDonald
Bagneux 1990

also draws, for example 76 ♖d6
♖xd6 77 exd6 ♔d7 78 ♔e5 ♔d8!
79 ♔xe6 ♔e8; however, White can
play 76 ♖h2 followed by ♖h7, ♖e7
and ♖xe6 when Black cannot exchange rooks since, as we know
from chapter One, the pawn endgame would be lost for him. Thus
Black prefers to give up the pawn
straight away and speed up the
drawing process) **76 ♖a2 ♖e3**
(Black knows his rook is in its
best position so he waits calmly)
**77 ♖a8+ ♔d7 78 ♖a7+ ♔e8 79
♔xe6 ♔f8!** (all as planned) **80
♖a8+ ♔g7 81 ♖d8** (if 81 ♔d6
♔f7! stopping the passed pawn's
advance; then after 82 ♖a7+ ♔e8
we have returned to square one)
81...♖e1 82 ♖d2 ♔f8! (preventing the king being cut off by 83
♖f2 is the simplest way to draw)
**83 ♖f2+ ♔e8 84 ♖h2 ♔f8 85
♖h5 ♖e2 86 ♖h1 ♖e3** and a draw
was finally agreed after another
26 moves.

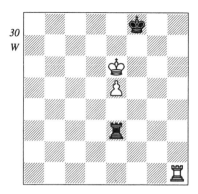

The last try was **87 ♖h8+ ♔g7
88 ♖e8**, defending the e-pawn
with the rook and so freeing the
king to play 89 ♔d7, but then
Black can draw with **88...♖a3!**
planning to give lots of checks or
play ...♔f7 when appropriate. If
White anticipates these checks
with **89 ♖d8**, then **89...♖e3!** and
we are back to our normal ways
since 90 ♔d7 is ruled out. If White
persists in this plan with **90 ♖d5**,
defending the pawn an alternative way, then **90...♔f8 91 ♔d7
♔f7** and the pawn is stymied.

**Rook and pawn on the seventh
against rook**

This is another tricky endgame
which it is well worth the reader
knowing.

Imagine if in Diagram 26 the
black rook were on a2 rather than
c2 (see following diagram).

Now White to move wins easily
with **1 ♖f1+ ♔g7 2 ♖f4**, building
his bridge, but Black to move
could try checking with **1...♖a8+**.

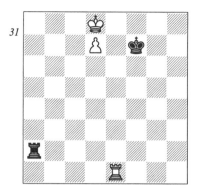

However, he loses after **2 ♔c7 ♖a7+ 3 ♔c8 ♖a8+ 4 ♔b7 ♖d8 5 ♔c7**. The white king can get close enough to the rook to end the checking sequence whilst at the same time not wandering too far from the passed pawn. But if we move all the pieces except the black rook one file to the right, then suddenly the verdict changes.

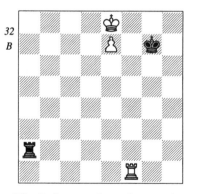

Black draws after the continuation **1...♖a8+ 2 ♔d7 ♖a7+ 3 ♔d8 ♖a8+ 4 ♔c7 ♖a7+ 5 ♔d6 ♖a6+ 6 ♔d5 ♖a5+ 7 ♔c6 ♖a6+ 8 ♔b7 ♖e6**.The white king can't approach Black's rook to end the checks without jeopardising his passed pawn.

The comparison of the two diagrams above provides us with a very important rule for such endgames. To have the best chance of drawing, the defender should try to get his rook on the "long" side of the passed pawn, i.e. the side with the most intervening squares between the pawn and the edge of the board. Moreover, his rook should be stationed on the most distant file on the long side. Conversely, the defender's king should if possible be placed on the short side, so it doesn't obstruct the action of his rook. Thus, in Diagram 31, the black king is on the long side and the black rook is on the short side of the board, and hence the rook is too close to the black king to draw. On the other hand, in Diagram 32, the black rook is on the long side, and he draws because he is at a sufficient distance from the white king.

However, we should point out that White often wins, even if the black rook is on the long side. Thus in diagram 32, if the white rook were on virtually any of the squares on the c- or d-files he would win by blocking the checks, e.g. with the white rook on d1, 1...♖a8+ 2 ♔d7 ♖a7+ 3 ♔e6 ♖a6+ 4 ♖d6 etc. One exception to this is the c6-square, since Black has the defence 1...♖a8+ 2 ♔d7 ♔f7.

Nevertheless, a consideration of this general rule will allow the reader to better judge on which side of the board to place his king and rook in more complicated positions.

Rook and rook's pawn against rook

M. Karstedt 1909

The white king is trapped in front of the pawn (note that the black rook has to keep control of the b-file; if Black to move played 1...♖a1? then 2 ♖b2! and 3 ♔b7 wins at once). The question is, can the king be freed without allowing the black king to reach c7, when the position will be completely drawn (we shall see below why this is the case)? Analysis will convince us that White wins (it makes no difference who moves first, since Black can only wait):

1 ♖c2 ♔e7 2 ♖c8 ♔d6 (even easier for White is 2...♔d7 3 ♖b8 ♖a1 4 ♔b7 ♖b1+ 5 ♔a6 ♖a1+ 6 ♔b6 ♖b1+ 7 ♔c5 and the king approaches the rook to kill the checking sequence) 3 ♖b8 ♖a1 4 ♔b7 ♖b1+ 5 ♔c8! (the only way out, since the black king bars the c5-square) 5...♖c1+ 6 ♔d8 ♖h1! (the best defence. Now both 7 a8♕?? ♖h8 mate and 7 ♖b6+ ♔c5 8 a8♕? ♖h8+ are not satisfactory for White) 7 ♖b6+ ♔c5 8 ♖c6+! (but this does the trick!) 8...♔d5 (obviously forced, and hoping for 9 ♖c8 ♔d6) 9 ♖a6 ♖h8+ 10 ♔c7 and White wins.

In Diagram 34, White's rook is trapped in front of the pawn and Black's rook is in an optimum position behind it. The position of Black's king is also superb. Black can draw by keeping his rook behind the pawn.

Should the white king approach the a-pawn to free his rook, then Black can drive it away by checking. For example, 1 ♔c6 ♖a2 2 ♔b6 ♖b2+! 3 ♔c6 ♖a2 4 ♔b7 ♖b2+ 5 ♔c6 ♖a2 and a draw is inevitable.

Note that if the black king were on a worse square then he would probably lose. For example, if it were on f7 then White to move could win with the trick 1 ♖h8! ♖xa7 2 ♖h7+ (a common tactical device in such endings), but if the black king were on f7 and it was Black to move, then he could draw with 1...♔g7!.

Here we end our brief examination of technical rook and pawn endgames. Even if he learns nothing else from the book, the reader should try to grasp the winning and drawing procedures in the above examples. This knowledge will undoubtedly save him some points and half-points in the future.

Now we will examine some other important technical endgames.

Queen against pawn on the seventh rank

35
B

The winning method is to force the white king in front of the pawn, so that there is temporarily

no longer a threat to queen. This gives Black time to edge his king closer, until he can mate or win the pawn.

Typical play from the diagram would be 1...♕a7+ 2 ♔f8 ♕b8+ 3 ♔f7 (not 3 ♔e7 ♕g8 winning at once) 3...♕f4+ 4 ♔e8 ♕g5 5 ♔f8 ♕f6+ 6 ♔g8 (the white king has been forced in front of the pawn, and now the black king can move one square closer) 6...♔c2 (now the process is repeated) 7 ♔h7 ♕f7 8 ♔h8 ♕h5+ 9 ♔g8 (again the king can move one square) 9...♔d3 (White will be mated in the end) 10 ♔f8 ♕f5+ 11 ♔e7 ♕g6 12 ♔f8 ♕f6+ 13 ♔g8 ♔e4 14 ♔h7 ♕f7 15 ♔h8 ♕h5+ 16 ♔g8 ♔f5 17 ♔f8 and now Black has many ways to win, perhaps the prettiest being 17...♔f6! 18 g8♕ ♕c5+ 19 ♔e8 ♕c8 mate.

As in many other endgames, the rook's pawn can be an exceptional case. If we move the g-pawn in Diagram 35 to h7, leaving the other pieces on the same squares, then Black to move wins with 1...♕h8, but White to move draws with 1 ♔g8! The point is that if Black employs the same winning procedure as for the g-pawn, he will stalemate White. Thus, 1 ♔g8 ♕a8+ 2 ♔g7 ♕g2+ 3 ♔h8! and Black cannot win since his king can only approach on pain of stalemate.

We are accustomed to the eccentricities of the rook's pawn, but it is surprising to learn that

White can also draws with the f-pawn. Thus imagine Diagram 35 with a white pawn on f7, not g7, and the white king on e7. Play could go 1...♕g7 2 ♔e8 ♕e5+ 3 ♔f8 ♔c2 (so far so good for Black) 4 ♔g8 ♕g5+ 5 ♔h8 ♕f6+ 6 ♔g8 ♕g6+ 7 ♔h8! (this is the point) and now Black can only draw by repetition with 7...♕h6+ 8 ♔g8 ♕g6+ 9 ♔h8 or stalemate White with 7...♕xf7.

Bishop and wrong colour rook pawn

The biggest weakness of the bishop is revealed in Diagram 36.

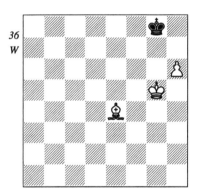

Since the bishop doesn't control the queening square of the rook's pawn, White cannot win despite his big material advantage. All he can do is stalemate Black's king after **1 h7+ ♔h8 2 ♔h6**. It is impossible to oust the king from the corner. Note that if White had a dark-squared bishop he would win easily by driving the black king from h8. In that case the rook's pawn would be the "right" rather than the "wrong" one.

This peculiar drawing feature regularly turns up in tournament games, so the reader needs to be aware of it.

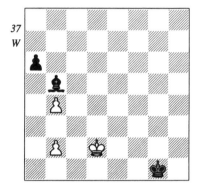

Ehlvest – Kasparov
Belgrade 1989

Without the doubled b-pawns White would be drawing easily. Kasparov's plan is to stalemate White's king and force him to play b5, when after ...axb5 Black has a b-pawn rather than an a-pawn. White has no defence against this plan. Play went:

93 ♔e1 ♔g2 94 ♔d1 ♔f3 95 ♔d2 ♔e4 96 ♔c3 ♔e3 97 ♔c2 ♔e2 98 ♔c1 ♗d3 99 b3 ♔e1 100 ♔b2 ♔d2 101 ♔a1 ♔c2 102 ♔a2 ♔c1

White has gradually been driven into the corner; if now 103 ♔a3, then 103...♔b1 104 ♔a4 ♔a2 105 ♔a5 ♔xb3 106 ♔b6 ♔xb4 followed by queening the pawn, since the white king has been pushed away. So Ehlvest tried

103 ♔a1

but resigned immediately after **103...♗b1!**

His king is stalemated and he is therefore forced into the hara-kiri 104 b5 when 104...axb5 105 b4 ♗d3 wins. Note that if White didn't have the b3-pawn then 104 b5 axb5 would be stalemate. Thus he lost solely because he had two b-pawns: with just one he would have drawn. Of course, Kasparov had it all planned from the middlegame!

Stalemate and perpetual check

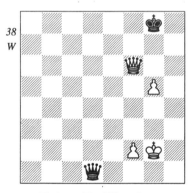

Pein – De Firmian
Bermuda 1995

White has two extra pawns. However, he is threatened with perpetual check by 65...♕g4+ 66 ♔f1 ♕d1+ 67 ♔g2 ♕g4+ 68 ♔h2 ♕h4+ etc. Of course, there are many ways to avoid it such as 65 ♕e6+ or 65 ♕f5. However, White

thought he had found the perfect answer:

65 g6?

We only give one question mark out of respect for the editor of *Chess Monthly* and also because there was something even more gruesome in the position: 65 ♔g3 ♕g1+ 66 ♔h4 ♕h2+ 67 ♔g4 ♕g2+ 68 ♔h5?? (activating the king) 68...♕h3+ 69 ♔g6 ♕h7 mate.

65 ...   ♕g4+
66 ♔h2

Malcolm Pein describes the situation in his magazine:

"Nick's arm reached out, I thought he was resigning but he was reaching for g2, not my sweaty palm..."

66 ...   ♕g2+!

and a draw was agreed.

Two knights can't win against a bare king

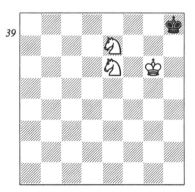

This has been described as one of the minor injustices of chess: two knights are a huge material advantage, and yet they can only stalemate in the absence of all other pieces and pawns. In fact, it would usually favour the attacker if his opponent had a pawn. In the diagram position, for example, the black king is trapped in the corner and 1 ♘g5 followed by 2 ♘f7 would mate if Black had a pawn on a7 or even a bishop on c3. Instead there is only stalemate.

It is sufficient that the reader is aware of the possibility of escaping from a bad position into this drawing haven, or equally avoids being duped into such a situation when he has the better chances. We do not plan to discuss here the extremely rare and complex endgame ♘+♘ v ♙.

Knights are weak against pawns

A knight can lose to a single passed pawn, especially when the pawn is supported by its king. The chances for the knight are especially bad against rook's pawns. This is because the knight only has half as many squares to work with compared with a centre pawn.

On the left hand side of the following diagram, White wins the knight with ♔c6 and ♔b7, and then queens his pawn. The knight is so feeble that it can't even sacrifice itself for the pawn.

On the right hand side of the diagram, the black pawn is only on the sixth rank and this, plus the ideal position of the knight, allows White to draw: 1 ♘f1+

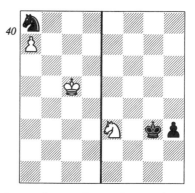

♔g2 2 ♘e3+ ♔f2 3 ♘g4+ ♔g3 4 ♘e3! A very important trick: the passed pawn cannot advance without White capturing it with 5 ♘f1+. Hence, Black is unable to drive away the knight and a draw results.

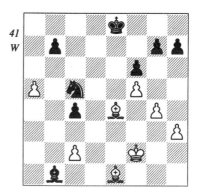

Anand – Lautier
London Intel 1995

Here Lautier has just attacked White's bishop with ...♘c5, no doubt expecting him to move it. He did so in style: Anand shot out **34 ♗xb7!** when after 34...♘xb7 35 a6 the a-pawn is unstoppable.

So Lautier tried **34...♔d7** but resigned after **35 ♗b4! ♔c7 36 ♗d5 ♘a6 37 c3 ♘xb4 38 cxb4 c3 39 ♔e3 ♔d6 40 ♗f3 h5 41 a6**.

Don't advance the a-pawn too quickly to a7! After 1 a7+ ♔a8 White cannot win. This is because he needs to use his knight to oust Black's king from a8 with ♘c7+. The only way he can free the knight from the defensive duty of guarding the a7-pawn is by playing ♔b6 or ♔a6, but both of these moves allow stalemate. Instead, there is an immediate win with **1 ♔b6 ♔a8 2 ♘c7+ ♔b8 3 a7+**.

Bishop and pawn versus bishop

With the defending king at some distance this is usually an easy win. The defending bishop is driven away and prevented from sacrificing itself for the pawn.

White won the following position after **72 ♗b6 ♗c3 73 ♗c7 ♗d4 74 ♗d6** (the standard manoeuvre, planning 75 ♗c5 to force

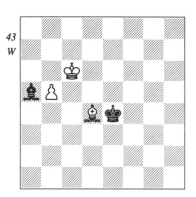

McDonald – Roberts
Hastings 1991

the advance of the pawn) **74...♗a7 75 ♗c5 ♗b8 76 b6 ♗g3 77 ♗d6 ♗f2 78 b7 ♗a7 79 ♔b5! ♔d5 80 ♔a6**. The bishop has finally been defeated in its attempt to hold up the pawn, so Black resigned.

Things are more difficult when the defender's king can attack the pawn. Some finesse is normally required.

Short – Korchnoi
Horgen 1995

In order to get his pawn past the hurdle on f3, Black carried a typical manoeuvre: **56...♔g3 57 ♔d2 ♗f3 58 ♗c4 ♗g4 59 ♗d5 ♗h3! 60 ♗e4 ♗g2 61 ♗d3 f3 62 ♔e3 f2 63 ♗c4 ♗d5 64 ♗f1 ♗c6!** Now White is in zugzwang. If 65 ♔e2, then 65...♗b5+ wins, so he must either play 65 ♔d2 allowing 65...♔h2 or move his bishop allowing 65...♔g2. In both cases the black king is able to reach the g1-square with a simple win. In the *British Chess Magazine* Chandler points out the elegant finish 65 ♗c4 ♔g2 66 ♗a6 ♔g1 67 ♗c4 ♗g2 68 ♗b5 ♗f1 69 ♗d7 ♗c4 70 ♗h3 ♗e6!

In the game Short simply resigned after 64...♗c6.

The next position is the most difficult example, and also the oldest: it was a study composed by Centurini in 1847.

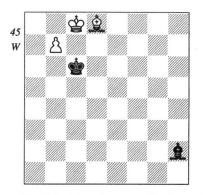

Black's king is so well placed that it is not clear how White can evict the bishop from the long diagonal. The natural attempt to get the bishop to b8 fails: 1 ♗h4 ♔b6! 2 ♗f2+ ♔a6 and Black's king has prevented 3 ♗a7 by going to a6. If White now tries to get his bishop to c7, the king follows him back again: 3 ♗h4 ♔b6 4 ♗d8+ ♔c6 and we are back to the diagram position. So is it a draw?

White would win if he could gain a tempo somehow in the above sequence. Then Black's king would not arrive in time to thwart his plan of ♗a7. This tempo can be gained by exploiting the necessity of the black bishop to stay on the long diagonal controlling b8.

White wins with **1 ♗h4 ♔b5 2 ♗f2 ♔a6 3 ♗c5!** (this forces the black bishop to move, or otherwise 4 ♗a7 wins) **3...♗g3 4 ♗e7 ♔b5 5 ♗d8 ♔c6.** Now we have reached the diagram position but with the black bishop on g3 rather than h2. This means that White can gain a vital tempo with **6 ♗h4!** when after **6...♗h2 7 ♗f2** Black can't get his king to a6 to rule out ♗a7. Now White wins as in the variation in Short-Korchnoi: **7...♗f4 8 ♗a7 ♗h2 9 ♗b8 ♗g1 10 ♗g3 ♗a7 11 ♗f2!**

Pawn against rook

A pawn can sometimes make a draw against a rook provided it is supported by its own king and the opponent's king is at a sufficient distance. Of course, the further advanced it is the better the drawing chances, assuming it is adequately protected.

McDonald – Mestel
London (Lloyds Bank) 1994

Black's passed pawns seem unstoppable after

45 ...   g3

but White found a way to simplify and draw:

46	hxg3	hxg3
47	Rxe2!	fxe2
48	Kxe2	g2
49	Rg6	Kh2
50	Kf2	Kh1

This gains a tempo on 50...Rf8+ 51 Ke3 g1♕+ 52 Rxg1 Kxg1 53 Kd4, but it's not enough to win.

51 Rxg2!

An important moment. At first it seems that 51 Ke3 is correct, but Black then has 51...Rh4! 52 b5 (52 Kf2 Rf4+! and 53...Rxb4) 52...g1♕+ 53 Rxg1+ Kxg1. Now the white king is cut off from the passed pawn and Black can win it with ...Rb4 next move. Even if the white king started on c3 in this

position Black would win by using his king, e.g. 54...Kg2 when if White ever pushes his pawn then it is lost: 55 b6 Rh6 56 b7 Rb6. This trick of cutting off the king from the pawn is very important. The defender has to ensure that the passed pawn advances with the support of the king.

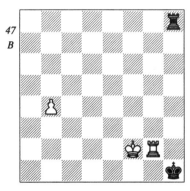

51	...	Rf8+
52	Ke3	Kxg2
53	Kd4	Kf3
54	b5	Rf5

Hoping for 55 b6? Rb5. The attempt to cut the king off from the pawn fails here since the pawn is too far advanced.

55	Kc4	Ke4
56	b6	Rf1
57	Kc5	Ke5
58	b7	Rb1
59	Kc6	

Here, without moving, Black offered a draw. I replied "maybe" watching the time on Mestel's digital clock counting down towards zero. With two seconds left for two moves he finally played

59 ...　　　　　　　Ïxb7
and yes, a draw was agreed!

Adams – Kramnik
Moscow (Olympiad) 1995

The game finished **52 bxa5? bxa5 53 ☖xd5 ☖f4 54 Ïa3** and a draw was agreed.

After the game Jon Speelman pointed out the win that White had missed. It runs 52 ☖xd5! ☖f4 53 Ïe1! and now Black has a choice of losing moves:

a) 53...☖f3 54 b5! g3 55 ☖c6 g2 56 ☖xb6 ☖f2 57 Ïa1 a4 58 ☖a5! a3 59 Ïa2+! ☖f1 60 Ïxa3 g1♛ 61 Ïa1+ wins. This variation shows why White should have avoided the exchange of pawns.

Black can also try eliminating White's pawn, but then he loses a crucial tempo which allows the white king to get back and stop the advance of the g-pawn:

b) 53...axb4 54 ☖d4! ☖f3 55 ☖d3 g3 (or 55...☖f2 56 Ïe2+! ☖f3 – trying to stop the white king's approach – 57 Ïe6 g3 58 Ïf6+

☖g2 59 ☖e2 and wins) 56 Ïf1+ ☖g2 57 ☖e2 ☖h2 58 Ïb1 b3 59 ☖f3 g2 60 Ïb2 and wins. Note that without the b-pawns Black could draw at the end of this line with 60...☖a1! 61 Ïxg2 stalemate.

Queen and pawn against queen

This type of endgame postpones prizegivings and closing ceremonies at tournaments across the world! Therefore it is appropriate to save it for last in this chapter.

The chances of winning this type of endgame gradually recede in proportion to the pawn's distance from the centre. With a well-advanced and supported central passed pawn and the opponent's king far away, it should be a win; with the f-pawn there are excellent winning chances; with the g-pawn it may be a win; and with the h-pawn it is much more problematical. The reason is that with a centre pawn the king has a much better chance of evading perpetual check.

Of course, the defender can usually give an excruciating number of checks. However, these checks normally run out at some point, either because his opponent has a winning line which evades the checks, or because the defender blunders through exhaustion and checks from the wrong square.

In the following diagram, we see a very favourable position for White. The pawn is already on the

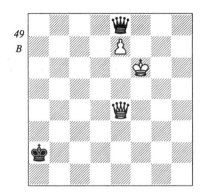

seventh rank and the king is at hand to support it. The white queen is well centralised and protects the pawn, while the black king is far off. With Black to play it could finish **1...♛h8+ 2 ♔f7 ♛h5+ 3 ♔e6** (intending 4 ♛a8+) **3...♛h3+ 4 ♛f5 ♛e3+ 5 ♔f7 ♛a7** (if 5...♛b3+, then 6 ♛e6!) **6 ♔f8 ♛a3 7 ♛f7+ ♔a1 8 ♔g8 ♛g3+ 9 ♛g7+!** and White forces the exchange of queens by utilising one of his most powerful weapons in this type of position: the cross-check.

Here we end our examination of technical positions. With this knowledge the reader should have nothing to fear in simple endgames.

3 Positional Themes

There is a well-known saying that the most difficult thing is to win a so-called "winning position". This applies not only in chess: in every sport it is common for a player on the brink of victory to suddenly and inexplicably collapse. He "gets the gripes" in golf, "hits the wall" in athletics or "chokes" in tennis. Often it happens to a player about to achieve an unexpected victory against a much stronger opponent. After doing everything right throughout the whole game, they slip up at the end. They simply can't finish off the game! Usually the breakdown is blamed on nerves and lack of experience in such situations, but one thing is clear: *the more you trust your winning technique, the less likely you are to be nervous and the more likely you are to win*

A sign of a truly great champion is how well he or she handles such situations. Players such as Kasparov and Karpov possess fine technique and always finish off their opponents with ruthless accuracy.

In this chapter we shall look at four positional themes and see how they can be applied to turn a "winning position" into a win. The themes are: exploiting weak pawns; the restraint of counterplay; the art of exchanging; and king activity.

Exploiting weak pawns

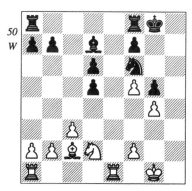

Smyslov – Ioseliani
Prague 1995

In our first example, the black d-pawns are among the weakest imaginable: doubled, isolated and on an open file. A wretched position to have against a veteran ex-World Champion!

There is something inexorable about the way Smyslov grinds out the win. He is in no hurry and it takes 15 moves for the first enemy d-pawn to fall. First of all, Black's counterplay is subdued, and only then does White begin to manoeuvre against Black's weak pawns – a good lesson in technique and patience from the venerable Grandmaster.

22 f3
Defending g4.
22 ...   a5!

If Black does nothing active then White will attack the d5-pawn in a direct manner, for example ♔f2, ♘f1 and ♘e3, ♗b3, or some other combination of moves involving the doubling of rooks along the d-file. The pawn would soon become indefensible, so Black must try for queenside counterplay.

23 ♘b3

Since 23 ♗b3 can be answered by ...a4, White begins by playing his knight to the brilliant outpost square on d4.

He also avoids playing a3, as this would allow Black to break up the queenside with ...b5 and ...b4. White doesn't want to be distracted from his task of attacking the d-pawns, and so prefers to keep his queenside as solid as possible. Thus, if Black tries ...a4 and ...a3, the reply b4 will keep the queenside intact. The tactics behind this are examined in the next note.

23 ... b5

In *Informator 64*, Vassily Smyslov analyses 23...a4 24 ♘d4 a3 25 b4 ♖ac8 26 ♖e3 ♖fe8 27 ♖d3 followed by ♗b3. The d5-pawn is then sooner or later doomed. Black cannot exploit the weakness of c3 nor can she profit through control of the e-file: there are no breakthrough points.

24 ♘d4 b4

Pursuing her policy of activity, despite the fresh weakness created on b4. But otherwise she has to await the loss of the d5-pawn and eventual defeat.

25 cxb4 axb4

Now at least the attack on a2 is some consolation for Black.

26 ♗d3!

With the plan of first fixing the pawn on b4 with b3 and then attacking it with ♘c2. After this has been implemented, the b4-pawn will be at least as weak as the white a-pawn, and a black rook will be tied down to its defence.

26 ... ♖fc8

27 ♔f2 ♖c5

28 b3! ♗c8?

Ioseliani should have played 28...♖ca5, attacking the a2-pawn. White would reply 29 ♖e2 and try to free his rook on a1 from its passive defensive duty. However, it is not clear how this can be done without allowing Black counterplay. In any case, it was Black's only chance.

29 ♘c2!

Now the black rook on a8 is forced to assume a defensive role defending b4. At the same time as this rook becomes passive, the white queen's rook gains its freedom.

29 ... ♖b8

30 ♖e2 ♖c3

Black cannot keep the rook on a1 inactive any longer. If 30...♖a5 31 ♘d4 (threat 32 ♘c6) 31...♖ba8 32 ♘c6 ♖a3 33 ♖b2 (not 33 ♘xb4 ♖xb3) and White wins the b4-pawn.

31 ♖d1 ♔g7

32 ♘d4

Back again, but the mission has been accomplished: White's rook now stands actively on d1.

32 ... ♘d7(?)

Simplification with 32...♖xd3 33 ♖xd3 ♗a6 was a better chance, getting rid of the inert black bishop. However, it's no wonder that Black crumbles under the pressure of a miserable defence.

33 ♖e8

Not 33 ♘b5 ♖xd3!, but now this really is threatened as the bishop on c8 will hang.

33 ... ♖a8

Attacking a2.

34 ♖d2 ♘e5
35 ♗e2 ♘c6

There was no good answer to the threat of 36 ♘b5. If instead 35...♗b7, then 36 ♖xa8 ♗xa8 37 ♘c2 ♘c6 38 ♗b5 ♘a7 39 ♗a4! winning b4.

36 ♘b5 d4
37 ♘xd6!

Winning. A player of Smyslov's understanding is not to be side-tracked by variations such as 37 ♘xc3?? bxc3 38 ♖c2 ♘b4. No chances to the opponent!

37 ... ♗b7
38 ♖xa8 ♗xa8
39 ♘b5 ♖c1
40 ♘xd4

Both d-pawns have fallen. The rest is silence.

40...♘e5 41 ♖c2 ♖a1 42 ♖c5 ♔f6 43 ♖a5 ♗b7 44 ♖a4 ♗d5 45 ♖a6+ ♔e7 46 ♘c2 ♖h1 47 ♘xb4 ♖h2+ 48 ♔e3 and Black resigned.

Ioseliani clearly believes that Smyslov has the technique to win three pawns up!

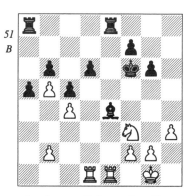

Archangelsky – Suetin
Biel 1994

If 26...♗xf3? 27 ♖xd6+. But Black found a clever way to seize the advantage.

26...d5! 27 cxd5?

Much too compliant. Although White temporarily wins a pawn, his pawn structure is reduced to rubble. It was better to play 27 ♘h2!? d4 (if 27...♗c2? 28 ♘g4+ ♔g7 29 ♖xe8 ♖xe8 30 ♖xd5 and White wins a pawn "cleanly" while if 27...dxc4 28 ♖d6+ ♔g7 29 ♖xb6 gives White counterplay) 28 ♘f1 followed by ♘d2, blocking the passed d-pawn and defending c4. White would face a difficult struggle to draw, but it was his best chance. The game continuation is hopeless.

27...♗xf3 28 ♖xe8 ♖xe8 29 gxf3 ♖d8 30 ♔g2 ♔e5 31 ♖e1+ ♔d6 32 f4

Here 32 b3 was the only chance.
32...c4 33 ♖e5 ♖c8
Intending ...♖c5 and ...♖xb5.
The white pawns, none of which
can defend each other, are easy
pickings for Black's king and
rook.
**34 ♔f3 c3 35 bxc3 ♖xc3+ 36
♔e4 ♖c4+ 37 ♔d3 ♖b4 38 ♖e8
♖xb5**
Now Black's connected passed
pawns must win.
**39 ♖d8+ ♔e7 40 ♖b8 a4 41 f5
a3 42 fxg6 fxg6**
White resigned. If 43 ♖a8 ♖xd5+
44 ♔c2 ♖a5 45 ♖xa5 bxa5 wins
easily in the pawn endgame.

Restraint of counterplay

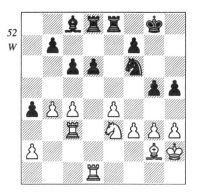

P. Nikolić – Kovalev
Tilburg 1993

White would win the d6 pawn
after 28 ♖cd3 e.g. 28...♖e6? 29 c5
♘e8 30 ♘f5. However, Black does
not have to defend passively. Instead, he can reply 28...g4! breaking up White's kingside. Then, in

view of the weakness of e4 and
White's fragmented pawn structure, it would be very hard for
White to prove his advantage.
So Nikolić remembered the principle "do not hurry!" and played
28 g4!
This prevents 28...g4 and so destroys Black's counterplay.
**28 ... hxg4
29 hxg4 ♔f8
30 ♔g3!**
Here White again avoids the lure
of immediate material gain. It
seems that 30 ♖a3 is very strong,
since 30...b5? 31 cxb5 cxb5 32 ♗f1
is very bad for Black: his pieces
are tied down to weak pawns on
b5 and d6 and White can penetrate down the c-file or double
rooks on the d-file.
However, Nikolić points out in
Informator 60 that Black can sacrifice the a-pawn with 30...♗e6!
If 31 ♖xa4, then 31...♖a8 gives
Black play along the a-file. There
could follow 32 ♖xa8 ♖xa8 33 ♖d2
♖a3 34 ♖e2 ♖a4 35 ♖b2 ♖a3 36
♖e2 ♖a4 with a draw.
White prefers to keep his opponent tied up.
**30 ... ♗e6
31 ♖cd3 ♔e7
32 f4!**
With his pieces on more or less
optimal squares, White decides it
is time to break open the position
and press for the win.
In return, Black is allowed to
activate his pieces somewhat, particularly his rook on e8 which

eventually reaches White's second rank. Doesn't this contradict what we have said about the need to restrain all counterplay? There is a chess expression, half joke and half aphorism that says: in order to win you have to give your opponent counterplay! The white advantage consists of his better co-ordinated pieces and superior pawn structure: notably Black has a weak pawn on d6 and a "hole" on f5 which cannot be defended by a pawn (White has a similar "hole" on e5, but it is impossible for Black to get his knight there to exploit it without losing the d-pawn). However, this advantage is hardly enough to win on its own. On the other hand, a well co-ordinated force, aided by the presence of targets, should outdo a disorganised one if the game opens up. Hence although both sides will gain activity through an opening of lines, White's pieces should prosper the most.

Rather than permitting Black counterplay, it could be said that White is forcing Black to come out from behind his defences and fight, and if it comes to a pitched battle the side with superior mobility should win. However, care is necessary with such an operation.

32	...	gxf4+
33	♔xf4	♖h8
34	♗f3	♖h2
35	a3	♖f2
36	♘f5+	♗xf5
37	exf5	

White's strategy has noticeably strengthened his game: in particular, the dormant bishop on f3 now has an open diagonal. Black no longer has a good defence against g5 and f6, when he will be overwhelmed.

37	...	♖g8
38	g5	♘h5+
39	♔e3	♖xf3+

The only defence to the four threats of 40 ♔xf2, 40 ♗xh5, 40 f6+ and 40 ♖xd6.

| 40 | ♔xf3 | ♖xg5 |

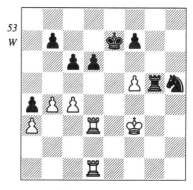

53
W

41 ♖xd6?

White has played excellently so far, but this is too greedy, too automatic! It is true that 41 ♔e4? ♖g4+ 42 ♔f3 ♖xc4 43 ♖xd6 ♘f6 gives Black good drawing chances, but there was a simple win with 41 ♖e1+! and now Black has the following possibilities:

a) 41...♔f6 42 ♖xd6+ ♔xf5 43 ♖e7 and Black's pawns will be decimated;

b) 41...♔f8 42 ♖xd6 ♖g3+ (or 42...♖xf5+ 43 ♔g4 ♘g7 44 ♖d8+

wins) 43 ♔f2 ♖xa3 44 f6 wins a
piece or mates; or

c) 41...♔d7 42 ♖de3 ♖xf5+ (or
Black has no counterplay) 43 ♔g4
♘g7 44 ♖e7+ ♔c8 45 ♖h1 and 46
♖h8 mates.

However, White's actual move
proves sufficient to win.

| 41 | ... | ♖g3+ |

According to Kovalev, the best
chance for Black was 41...♘f6
followed by ...♖xf5+, with some
drawing chances.

42	♔f2	♖xa3
43	c5	♖a2+
44	♔e3	♖a3+

After 44...♘f6 45 ♔d3 (threat
46 ♖e1+) 45...♘d5 46 f6+! ♔e8
(46...♘xf6 47 ♖e1+) 47 ♖e1+ Black
will be mated.

45	♔f2	♖a2+
46	♔e3	♖a3+
47	♔d4	♖f3
48	♖e1+	♔f8
49	♔e5	♔e7
50	♔d4+	♔f8
51	♔e5	♔e7
52	♖h1!	

Finally White finds the winning plan.

52	...	f6+
53	♔d4	♖f4+
54	♔c3	♖xf5
55	♔b2!	

A patient move. The white king
heads off after the a-pawn and so
destroys Black's counterplay. The
black king, meanwhile, has no
role beyond that of target – it
could easily be mated by the
white rooks.

55	...	♔f7
56	♔a3	♔g6
57	♔xa4	♘g3
58	♖e1	♖f2
59	♔a5	♖b2
60	♖g1!	♖b3
61	♖d7	

Only now does White go after
the b7-pawn. Black's last chance
rests with his f-pawn.

61	...	f5
62	♖xb7	f4
63	b5	cxb5
64	♖xb5	♖xb5+
65	♔xb5	♔f6
66	c6	♘f5
67	c7	♘e7
68	♔c5	

and Black resigned. Both 68...f3
69 ♖f1 and 68...♔e6 69 ♖e1+ intending 70 ♖xe7 are hopeless for
him.

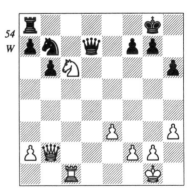

Kramnik – Lutz
Germany 1994

The black queenside pawns are
restrained by the pressure of the
white pieces and can only advance

on pain of capture. This in turn affects the co-ordination of the black pieces, because the rook dare not leave a8. The question now is whether the game ends in a quick draw or becomes unremitting torture for Black. Black to move could escape from the bind with 27...♘c5! when ideas of 28...♕xc6 or 28...♘d3 would force the knight on c6 to retreat, but it is Kramnik's move (funny how it always seems to be his move at the critical point!) and he found a way to keep Black constricted:

27 ♕d4!

This offer to exchange queens is very unpleasant for Black. If 27...♕xd4 28 exd4! when White has a passed pawn and the knight on b7 is denied c5. Black has problems, e.g. 28...♔f8? (28...♘d6!) 29 ♘e5 followed by 30 ♖c7 with a clear advantage to White.

27 ...   ♘c5?

In fact Black had a chance to equalise. In *Informator 60*, Kramnik recommends 27...♕e6! (attacking a2) 28 ♕c4 ♕e8! persistently avoiding the exchange of queens. Then next move Black can play ...♘c5 with equality.

28 ♕xd7   ♘xd7
29 ♖d1   ♘c5
30 g4!

Beginning the standard procedure in such positions: the advance of the pawn majority. Black cannot easily free his rook from defensive duty on a8, because advancing either queenside pawn

creates a serious structural weakness.

30 ...   g6?

Here 30...b5? 31 ♖d5 wins a pawn. The alternative 30...a5?! looks terrible, but maybe isn't so bad, e.g. 31 ♖b1 ♘a4!? At least the rook would be freed from its passive role.

The natural move was 30...♔f8. But after 31 ♔g2 Black is struggling, e.g.:

a) 31...♖c8? 32 ♘xa7 ♖a8 loses to 33 ♘c6 ♖xa2? 34 ♖d8 mate.

b) 31...♔e8 32 h4 ♘e6 (but not 32...♖c8? 33 ♘xa7 as in line a) 33 h5 and after both 33...♘d8 34 ♘d4 intending 35 ♘f5 and 33...♖c8 34 ♖d6!? ♖c7 35 f4!? intending f5 White has a clear advantage.

Black's actual move creates a weakness on the kingside which eventually proves fatal.

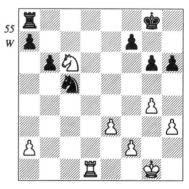

31 ♔g2   ♔g7

Black hopes to equalise with 32...♖c8 33 ♘xa7 ♖a8 34 ♘c6 ♖xa2. Kramnik, of course, puts a stop to the idea.

32 ♖d2!   a6

Now b6 is weakened, but Black cannot afford to play without his rook any longer: White was threatening to slowly increase the pressure with f4, ♔f3, e4, e5, etc.

33 ♖d6!

This is the perfect position for the rook, as will be revealed.

33 ...   ♖c8

34 ♘d4   b5

35 h4!

Now Kramnik's plan begins to unfold. He will play h5, when if Black responds ...gxh5 or ...g5, then ♘f5 (+) will be very strong. If, after h5, Black maintains his pawn on g6, then White plays hxg6. The recapture ...fxg6 will then leave White with a passed pawn on e3 which will win the game, unless Black somehow succeeds in generating counterplay with his queenside pawns.

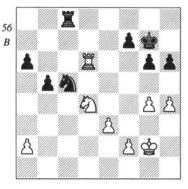

35 ...   b4

So Lutz advances his pawns immediately. He loses a pawn, but there was no good alternative.

36 ♖b6   a5

37 ♖b5

White finally wins his pawn, but technical difficulties remain.

37 ...   ♘d3

38 ♖xa5   ♘e1+

39 ♔g3   ♘c2

40 ♘b3

Of course White avoids the exchange of knights – all rook and pawn endgames are drawn! However, Kramnik points out that 40 ♘f3 was even better, planning 41 ♘e5 and an attack on f7.

40 ...   ♘a3

41 ♖a4   ♖c4

42 ♘d4!

Kramnik realises his knight belongs on f3 and so retracts his 40th move. No foolish pride stops him from admitting his mistake!

42 ...   ♘c2

43 ♘f3   ♖c5

Keeping the knight out of e5.

44 ♖a7   g5

This move leaves a fatal hole on f5, which White soon exploits. The only chance was 44...♘a3 45 g5 h5 (Kramnik). However, White should win comfortably e.g. 46 ♘d2 ♖c2 (46...♖e5 47 ♖b7!?) 47 ♘e4 ♔f8 (47...♖xa2 48 ♖a8! b3 49 ♘f6 mates) 48 ♖b7 (intending 49 ♖xb4 or 49 ♘d6) 48...♖xa2 49 ♖xb4 ♘c2 50 ♖b7 and there is no answer to the threat of ♘d6 winning f7.

45 h5

Now White has only to put his knight on f5 and the game will be over.

45	...	♔g8
46	♘d2	♘a3
47	♘e4	♖c2
48	♖b7	

The safest way to win: with the disappearance of b4 Black has no counterplay.

48	...	♖xa2
49	♖xb4	♖c2
50	♖b6	♔h7
51	♖b7!	

Accuracy to the end! Here 51 ♘d6 may look decisive, but Kramnik had noticed that 51...♘c4! 52 ♖c6 ♘xe3! saves Black.

| 51 | ... | ♔g8 |
| 52 | ♘d6 | |

Only now!

52	...	♖c6
53	♘xf7	♘c4
54	♖d7	♖f6
55	♖d4	

and Black resigned. If 55...♘xe3 56 ♘xh6+ wins, while after any other move the knight on f7 escapes.

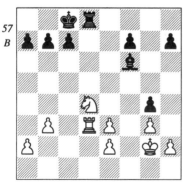

57
B

Claesen – M.Gurevich
Antwerp 1994

Black has the better minor piece and a healthy queenside pawn majority, whereas White's doubled and isolated e-pawns are a serious weakness. Therefore Black clearly has all the chances. He only has to be careful that his kingside pawns, which are somewhat fragmented and on light squares, do not become vulnerable to attack by the white knight.

23 ...   ♖d5!

The first move in a campaign to restrict the activity of the white knight. He begins by preventing ♘f5, when after ♘h6 both f7 and g4 would be attacked.

24 h3

The attempt to gain counterplay with 24 ♖d1 c5 (24...♗g5!?) 25 ♖f1 fails after 25...cxd4 26 ♖xf6 dxe3 27 ♖xf7 ♖d2 and Black should win.

24 ...   h5!

Much better than the alternative 24...gxh3+. Black keeps the white king penned in by denying it access to f3.

| 25 | hxg4 | hxg4 |
| 26 | a4 | c6! |

Now he rules out 27 ♘b5 when in view of the attack on a7 Black would be obliged to swap rooks with ...♖xd3, straightening out White's pawn structure.

27 ♔f2   a6

Preparing to bring in the king via c7 and b6 to c5 without being harassed by ♘b5+. Although restricted, we should recall that the knight is nicely centralised on d4, so Black would like to drive it back.

28 ♔g2

White decides he has his best set-up and so waits. The king cannot leave the kingside because of the weakness on g3.

28 ... ♔c7
29 ♖d1 ♗e5!

Also tempting is the variation 29...c5!? 30 ♘b5+ ♔c6 31 ♖xd5 (after the knight raid 31 ♘a7+ ♔d6 32 ♘c8+ ♔e6 33 ♖xd5 ♔xd5 34 ♘b6+ ♔c6 35 ♘c4 b5 Black is a tempo up on 31 ♖xd5) 31...♔xd5 32 ♘a3 ♔c6 intending ...b5. Black will then create a queenside passed pawn which should win the game.

In the game after 29 ♖d1, White is tied up and can do nothing constructive. Why, then, should Black force things when it is possible to build up his game gradually at no risk?

30 ♖h1

An attempt to achieve counterplay. Again Black has the chance to force things, this time with 30...♗xd4 31 exd4 ♖xd4. Play could then continue 32 ♖h7 ♖b4 33 ♖xf7+ ♔d6 (33...♔d8!?) 34 ♖f4 ♖xb3 35 ♖xg4 b5 36 axb5 axb5 37 ♖e4 c5 38 g4 c4 39 g5 ♖a3 and Black wins. However, not surprisingly Black prefers to steer clear of rook endgames with their notorious complexity. Why should he go for a forcing variation when he can increase the pressure with methodical play? White cannot escape!

30 ... ♔b6
31 ♖h7 ♖d7
32 ♘c2!

A clever defensive move. He prepares to meet 32...♖d2 by 33 ♘a3! when 33...♖xe2+?? 34 ♔f1 leaves Black facing both 35 ♔xe2 and 35 ♘c4+, winning the bishop. It would be surprising, though, if a tactical trick could overturn all Black's positional advantages.

32 ... ♗c3!
33 ♔f2 ♔c5

Black intends 34...b5 followed by 35...♖d2 36 ♘a3 ♗b2 37 ♘b1 ♖d1, winning the knight.

Therefore White tries to create some space, but the result is that the d4 bastion vanishes forever.

34 e4 ♖d2
35 ♖h5+ ♔d6
36 ♘a3

If 36 ♘e1, then 36...♗d4+ 37 ♔f1 ♖d1 is overwhelming, while 36 ♘e3 ♗d4 is a gruesome pin.

36 ... b5

All according to the restriction theme.

37 axb5 axb5
38 ♖xb5!?

A sacrifice which cannot save the day, but in view of the threat 38...♗b4 39 ♘b1 ♖b2 it was the only way to battle on.

38 ... cxb5
39 ♘xb5+ ♔e5
40 ♘xc3 ♔d4

The technical phase begins. The first stage of the winning plan is simple: capture the indefensible b3-and e4-pawns.

41	♘d5	♔xe4
42	♘e3	f5
43	♘g2	♖b2
44	♘f4	♖xb3

As the next step, Black forces the knight away from the f4-square. How this is to be done is soon revealed.

| 45 | ♘e6 | ♖a3 |
| 46 | ♘f4 | ♖a5 |

Defending f5 and so freeing the black king.

| 47 | ♘g2 | ♔d4 |

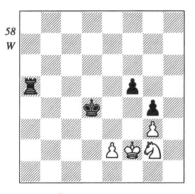

58
W

48 ♘h4

White's knight is compelled to take a different route. If he continues with 48 ♘f4, then Black will play ...♖e5 (restricting White's king) and put his king on d2 (if White tries to prevent this with ♔e1, then playing ...♔c2 and ...♖e3 will force ♘h5, when ...♔c1 puts White in zugzwang and gains access to d2). Once the king is on d2, playing ...♖e3 with White's king on f2 and his knight on f4 puts White in zugzwang: he would have to play ♔g2 when ...♖xe2+

gives White a winning pawn endgame. An alternative winning method would be to play ...♖e5, put the king on d2 (as above) but then continue ...♖e4, timed for when the knight is on f4. Then once again White would be in zugzwang, since Black can meet ♔f1 by ...♖xf4+ followed by ...♔e3 and ...♔xf4 with a winning pawn endgame.

So White sets up a second line of defence with the knight on h4.

48 ...   ♖e5!

If 48...♔c3 then 49 ♔e3! followed by ♔f4 escapes with a draw. The white king must be kept boxed in.

| 49 | ♘g6 | ♖e6 |
| 50 | ♘h4 |

If 50 ♘f4 Black wins as outlined at move 46, beginning with 50...♖e4 and 51...♔c3. However, White has found a more promising defensive set-up. He attacks the black rook with ♘g6 when it is on e5; if it retreats backwards he attacks the pawn on f5 with ♘h4 and if it goes sideways (say ...♖a5) then he is poised to answer ...♔c3 with ♔e3 and ♔f4, drawing easily. So how can Black win? To do so, he needs to devise a second, more complex, winning plan. Step by step, it can be outlined as follows:

a) Achieve ...♔d2 without losing the f-pawn. White will try to prevent ...♔d2 with ♔e1. So Black will have to drive away the white king with ♖a1+. This move has to be timed for when the knight is on g2, not h4, otherwise the f5-pawn will be hanging.

b) Once a is achieved, with the black king on d2 and the knight on h4 Black will win the e-pawn with ...♖e5; with the knight on f4, Black will win as outlined at move 42.

c) Therefore White's only defensive try is to play ♘g2 and ♘e3 when the black king has left d4. Then if ...♚d2, ♘f1+ drives the black king back.

d) However, when the knight goes to f1 to drive back/keep out the black king, it will be a long way from the f4-square. Black can therefore race back with his king to e5 and break through with the pawn advance ...f4 before the knight is able to return to g2 to cover this square.

e) After the advance ...f4 and gxf4 ♚xf4, Black will have a winning endgame by forcing through the g-pawn.

50 ...   ♚c3!

Black leaves the f-pawn undefended for a move, since 51 ♘xf5 ♖f6 52 e4 ♚d3 53 ♚g2 (forced) 53...♚xe4 54 ♘h4 ♚e3 wins easily (Gurevich).

51 ♚e1

He must stop 51...♚d2. Now 52 ♘xf5 is really a threat, but Black has gained a vital move by temporarily leaving the f-pawn undefended, as will be seen.

51 ...   ♖e5
52 ♘g2

If 52 ♘g6 then 52...♖a5 and because 50...♚c3 has forced the white king to e1, he no longer has the drawing possibility of ♚e3: Black has gained a crucial tempo so that 53 ♚f2 can be answered with 53...♚d2! keeping the white king out of e3.

52 ...   ♚c2
53 ♘h4   ♖b5
54 ♘g2   ♖b3
55 ♘h4

Black was hoping for 55 ♚f2? ♚d2, winning easily, but White isn't obliging and the exchange 55...♖xg3 56 ♘xf5 allows White to escape with a draw. Therefore Gurevich repeats the position and reverts to the methodical plan explained at move 50. It was worth trying 55...♖b3, just to see if White blundered. Nothing has been lost.

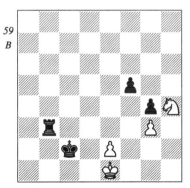

59
B

55 ...   ♖b5
56 ♘g2   ♖b1+
57 ♚f2   ♚d2

All as planned.

58 ♘e3

We already know what happens if White redeploys his knight to f4: 58 ♘h4 ♖b5 59 ♘g2 ♖e5 60 ♘f4 ♖e4! is zugzwang and Black wins the pawn endgame after 61 ♔f1 ♖xf4+ 62 gxf4 ♔e3 and 63...♔xf4.

So the knight has to take a different route, and loses touch with the f4-square.

58 ...   ♖b5

Of course not 58...♖e1? 59 ♘c4+ drawing.

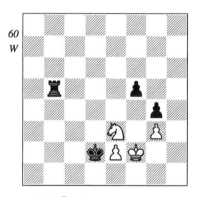

60
W

59 ♘c4+

A critical moment.

If 59 ♘f1+ ♔c3 60 ♔e3 ♖e5+ 61 ♔f2 (if 61 ♔f4 ♖xe2 62 ♘e3 ♔d3 63 ♘xf5 ♖e4+ 64 ♔g5 ♔e2 intending ...♔f3 wins) 61...♔d4 62 ♘d2 ♖e6!! (the only square which wins) 63 ♘f1 ♔e4 and now:

a) 64 ♘e3 f4! wins the knight after both 65 gxf4 g3+ and 65 ♘xg4 ♖g6 66 ♘h2 fxg3+. Note if at move 62 Black had played 62...♖e7 then now there would be the defence 65 ♘xg4 ♖g7 66 ♘f6+ ♔f5 67 ♘h5, while 62...♖e8 would be even worse since it allows a

knight fork on f6 if Black followed this sequence.

b) 64 ♘d2+ ♔e5 65 ♘c4+ (if 65 ♔e3, then 65...♔f6+ intending 66...♔g5 and 67...f4) 65...♔d4 66 ♘d2 ♖d6 67 ♔e1 ♖h6 68 ♘f1 f4! 69 gxf4 ♔e4 70 e3 ♔f3 and 71...g3 wins.

59 ...   ♔c3

60 ♘d6

White tires of his passive defence. If 60 ♘e3 ♖e5 the both knight retreats lose: 61 ♘g2 ♔d2 62 ♘f4 ♖e4 is our standard win (see note at move 48), while if 61 ♘f1 then Black completes the plan revealed at move 50: 61...♔d4 (stopping 62 ♘e3) 62 ♔e1 ♖a5 63 ♔f2 ♖a3! (again 64 ♘e3 is prevented) 64 ♔e1 ♔e5 65 ♔f2 f4 and wins (variation by Gurevich in *Informator 61*).

60...♖d5 61 ♘e8 ♔d2 62 ♘f6 ♖e5 63 e4 fxe4 64 ♘xg4 ♖f5+

and here White resigned as the e-pawn runs through. A fine technical display by Gurevich.

The art of exchanging

Throughout a game both players have to decide about which pieces to exchange and which to keep. Sometimes this task is obvious and straightforward, but at other times it demands a subtle appreciation of the position; then the greatest players can go wrong, as we shall see.

We begin with a simple example.

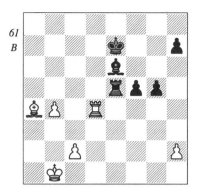

V. Palciauskas – E. Bang
Correspondence 1984-87

36 ...   ♖d5!
Forcing the exchange of rooks, after which the white king is too far away to halt the advance of Black's kingside pawns.

37 c3
If 37 ♖c4?, then 37...♖d1+ wins at once. 37 ♖xd5 ♗xd5 is also hopeless. The black pawns are irresistible, for example 38 ♔c1 f4 39 ♔d2 g4 40 ♔e1 h5 41 ♗b5 h4 42 c4 ♗e4 43 c5 g3 44 hxg3 h3! (easiest) and the h-pawn queens. This variation shows that after recapturing on d5 the black bishop controls a key diagonal.

37 ...   ♖xd4
38 cxd4
The white split passed pawns are no match for Black's kingside pawn mass. The game concluded **38...♗d5 39 ♔c1 h5 40 ♔d2 h4 41 ♗d1 g4 42 ♔e3 g3 43 h3 f4+** and White resigned.

Here it was easy to evaluate the position as winning for Black after 36...♖d5. The difficulty is to see such a move in the first place! But often the problem of exchanging requires a very sophisticated judgement. Next we see Kasparov solving a difficult problem.

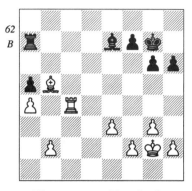

Kasparov – Portisch
Brussels 1986

White is two pawns up, but the opposite-coloured bishops make it hard for him to exploit his advantage. In such cases, the normal winning technique is to create a passed pawn on the queenside, beginning with b4, but here the b4-square is an impenetrable barrier as long as the black bishop stays on the a3-f8 diagonal. This virtually negates White's pawn plus on the queenside. However, White is also a pawn up on the kingside, and there is nothing to stop him gaining space there. The fact that the black bishop has to stay guarding b4 against a White breakthrough will make it less capable of defending the kingside.

If Black does nothing, White plans the pawn advances e4, e5 and f4, the centralisation of his king on e4, and then the further pawn advances g4 and f5, when Black will be gradually suffocated. So Black to move tried

44 ...   f5

Gaining some space and frustrating the white plan outlined above. However, it is not surprising that White has another way to increase his advantage.

45 h3!

Such unpretentious moves often win games.

45 ...   h5
46 g4!

Kasparov analyses this game in *The Brussels Encounter* (Chequers Chess Publications, 1987). There he points out that it seems strange to exchange two pawns when you are material up in the endgame. The normal advice is to exchange pieces, not pawns, since every pawn exchange brings the defender nearer to the refuge of a drawn pawnless endgame (e.g. a king and a bishop cannot win against a king: it is better to be left with a king and a pawn that you can try to queen). However, there are three good reasons why a double pawn exchange is good for White here:

a) White clears the way for his e-pawn, which becomes a passed pawn.

b) The g6-pawn, which is the weakest point in Black's kingside structure, becomes susceptible to a double attack by ♖c6 and ♗d3 once the f5-pawn has disappeared.

c) White's king gains an excellent square on g4, where it can assist in the advance of the kingside pawns or perhaps even join in the attack on g6.

46 ...   hxg4
47 hxg4   fxg4
48 ♔g3   ♗d6+
49 ♔xg4   ♖c7
50 ♗c6!

If 50 ♖xc7+?? ♗xc7 and Black puts his bishop on b4, answers ♔g5 with ...♗e7+ and should draw easily. Under no circumstances should White enter a pure opposite-coloured bishop endgame, unless it is a trivial win (and even then it may not prove so trivial!).

A great player such as Kasparov may once or twice a decade have a lapse and blunder a piece, but he would never exchange rooks in such a position, unless he needed a draw to keep his World Championship title!

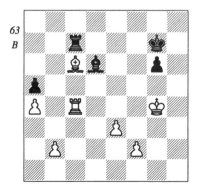

63
B

50 ...	**♖f7**
51 f4	**♔h6**
52 ♗d5	**♖f6**
53 ♖c1	

White is in no hurry. Portisch is left to suffer in his miserable position. It is no surprise that he eventually blunders and saves White the task of proving if he has a forced win.

53...♔g7 54 b3 ♖f8 55 ♖d1 ♗c5 56 ♖d3 ♗a3 57 ♗c4 ♗c1 58 ♖d7+ ♔h6 59 ♖e7 ♗d2 60 ♔f3 ♗b4 61 ♖b7 ♗c3 62 ♗d3 ♖f6 63 ♔g4 ♗d2 64 f5! and Portisch resigned. If 64...♗xe3 65 fxg6 ♖f4+ 66 ♔g3 intending both 67 ♖h7+ and 67 g7.

In the following example, Black made an instructive error which deprived him of a win. A lesson in "the art of exchanging unwisely"!

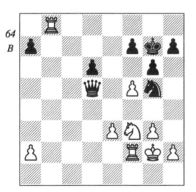

I. Farago – Adorjan
Hungary 1995

34 ...	**♕xf5?**

Allowing the trade of knights.

It is well known that a queen and a knight are a potent attacking force in the endgame. This is because they complement each other, possessing the combined power of every piece. A queen and a bishop, on the other hand, are generally less powerful since they "duplicate" the ability to move diagonally and lack the knights "x-ray" ability to look through enemy barriers. Also, in positions where the queen faces her material equivalent in several enemy pieces, but no enemy queen, she is generally more effective when she has some other pieces to aid her.

Bearing this in mind, Adorjan's decision must be criticised. After the correct 34...♘e4! 35 ♖fb2 ♕xf5 White would face serious problems in view of Black's attacking chances against his weakened king.

35 ♘xg5!	

Not missing his chance.

35 ...	**♕xg5**
36 ♖b3!	

Defending e3 and preparing to regroup his pieces. 36 ♖b7? ♕d5+ would be foolish.

36 ...	**♕d5+**
37 ♔g1	**♕c5**

Better was 37...a5 (Adorjan) for example 38 ♖c3 f5 followed by ...a4 and the centralisation of the black king. White would then find it difficult to organise his rooks to attack the d6-pawn while at the same time keeping e3 defended.

38 ♖d3!	

Now White can double rooks against d6.

38	...	♛c1+
39	♔g2	♛c6+
40	♔g1	♔f8
41	♖fd2	♔e7
42	h4!	

Of course, a pawn endgame after 42 ♖xd6?? ♛xd6 43 ♖xd6 ♔xd6 would be losing for White in view of his weak e-pawn and the more advanced black king. This is one exchange White should avoid!

The reader may wonder why White weakens his kingside with 42 h4. The point is he wants to build a fortress with the set-up of pawns on a4, e3, g3 and h4, rooks on d4 and d2, and king on f2. Then everything is secure and self-defending, but if he plays 42 ♔f2 immediately, then 42...g5! (42...♛h1 43 h4!) rules out 43 h4 and leaves White vulnerable to ...♛h1. In other words, with 42 h4 White prevents Black gaining space with ...g5.

Note that White can ignore any considerations of king safety in planning his fortress set-up. This is because the black queen on its own cannot strike a fatal blow. On the other hand, if Black had avoided the exchange of knights at move 34, then advances such as 42 h4? would have seriously jeopardised the white king's safety: a black knight would have rejoiced to see the holes on e4, f3, g4, and h3. Thus we can conclude that if Black had kept the knights on the board, White's defensive strategy would have been prevented and he would soon have faced defeat.

42	...	h6
43	♔f2	f5
44	♖d4	a5
45	a4!	

Preventing Black gaining any space with 45...a4.

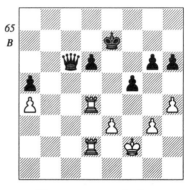

65
B

45	...	♔e6
46	g4!	

This tidies things up on the kingside. How Black would love to have a knight to exploit the weaknesses!

46...fxg4 47 ♖xg4 ♔f5 48 ♖gd4 ♔e5 49 ♔g3 ♛c5 50 ♖2d3 d5 51 ♖d2 ♛c6 52 ♖2d3 ♔e6 53 ♔f3 ♛b7

and Black tried for another 14 moves before giving up his winning attempt.

Errors of omission can be just as costly in the realm of exchanging. In the following game, Black mistakenly avoids an exchange which would free his game.

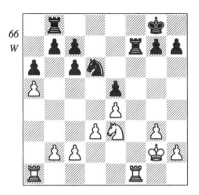

Ivanchuk – Short
Amsterdam 1994

White has a clearly superior pawn structure: e5 is weak and the black queenside pawns are constricted.

25 h4!

White aims to gain space on the kingside...

25 ...   ♖e8

...and Black does nothing to oppose him. In *Informator 60*, Ivanchuk recommends the alternative 25...♖bf8, planning multiple exchanges on f1. We can analyse 26 ♘g4 ♖xf1 27 ♖xf1 ♖xf1 28 ♔xf1 ♘f7 29 ♔e2 ♔f8 30 ♔e3 (planning to create a passed pawn with 31 d4) 30...c5! 31 c3 (31 ♔e2 ♔e7 32 ♘e3 ♔e6 33 ♘f5 g6 is also equal) 31...♔e7 32 d4 cxd4+ 33 cxd4 exd4+ 34 ♔xd4 ♔e6 and Black has nothing to fear.

This is a good illustration of the problem of exchanging. It was by no means obvious that Black's best method of defence involved a double rook exchange. With an inferior pawn structure, Black naturally feels that he should keep at least one rook on the board to help defend his weaknesses, but in the game, it is the presence, not the absence, of a rook that leads to Black's defeat. White gains control of the f-file and then seizes the seventh rank, all because Black wants to avoid the exchange of the last rook.

26 g4   ♘b5
27 ♖xf7   ♔xf7
28 ♖f1+   ♔e6
29 ♘f5   ♖g8

Without the rooks Black would have good drawing chances in this position.

30 g5   c5
31 c3

Now it is White's turn to choose the wrong plan. He should have played 31 h5!, continuing his plan of gaining space on the kingside. Then Ivanchuk analyses 31...♘d4 32 ♘xd4+ cxd4 33 g6 hxg6 34 hxg6 ♖e8 35 ♔g3 as "slightly better for White". Certainly it would be a most unpleasant position for Black to defend!

31 ...   ♘a7!
32 ♘e3   ♘c8?

Better was 32...♘c6! and the attack on a5 would frustrate the white attack, e.g. 33 ♘d5 ♖c8 (Ivanchuk).

33 h5   ♘e7

Now Black seems to have everything covered. However, Ivanchuk finds a killing pawn sacrifice.

34 ♘d5!   ♘xd5

There is no refusing, since 34...♖c8 fails after 35 h6 ♘xd5 (35...gxh6 36 ♖f6+ ♔d7 37 ♖f7 ♖e8 38 gxh6 ♔e6 39 ♖xh7 etc.) 36 exd5+ ♔xd5 37 hxg7 ♖g8 38 ♖f7.

35 exd5+   ♔xd5
36 ♖f7

The rook is completely dominant on the seventh rank. Black can only rue that he didn't exchange it off when he had the chance.

36 ...   b6

Passive defence would allow White to bring up his king, e.g. 36...♔c6 37 ♔f3 ♔d6 38 ♔e4 and now Black can only move pawns. The well-placed white pieces and far advanced kingside pawns mean that he wins any pawn race between the flanks e.g. 38...b6 39 c4 bxa5 40 b3 ♖b8 (if 40...c6 41 ♔f5 {zugzwang} 41...g6+ 42 ♔g4) 41 ♖xg7 ♖xb3 42 ♖xh7 ♖b1 (or 42...a4 43 g6 a3 44 g7 a2 45 g8♕ a1♕ 46 ♕d5 mate) 43 g6 ♖g1 44 g7 a4 45 ♖h6+! ♔e7 46 ♖g6! (a motif well worth remembering) 46...♖xg6 47 hxg6 and wins.

37 ♖xc7   bxa5
38 ♔f3   ♖f8+

The counterattack 38...♖b8 39 ♖xg7 ♖xb2 40 ♔e3 is much too slow.

39 ♔e3 h6 40 ♖xg7 hxg5 41 ♖xg5 ♖f4 42 c4+ ♔c6 43 ♖g6+ ♔b7 44 b3 ♖h4 45 h6 e4 46 dxe4 ♖h3+ 47 ♔f4 ♖xb3 48 ♖g3!

and Black resigned. If 48...♖b1 49 ♖h3 ♖f1+ 50 ♔e5 ♖f8 51 h7 ♖h8 52 ♔f6 and 53 ♔g7 wins.

King activity

The king is a strong piece: use it!
Reuben Fine

In the endgame the king becomes a fighting piece. It no longer has to cower behind its defences, trembling at even the shadow of an enemy piece. Instead it can put on its hiking boots and roam the board at will, gobbling up any loose pawns it finds, and perhaps helping to queen one or two pawns of its own. There are many examples of the king's power in this book. Here we shall concentrate on some startling examples in which the sudden entry of the king overwhelms a hard-pressed defence.

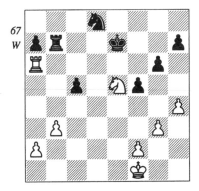

67
W

A position from one of the author's games. White evidently has a clear advantage. The black rook is tied down to the a7-pawn, the knight on d8 dare not move on account of ♘c6+ winning the a-pawn and the black king cannot approach the queenside to free his pieces. Consequently Black is tied up, but the question is, how can White win without giving Black any chances for activity? The answer is by using his king to overstretch Black's defence. Play continued **40 ♔e2!** **♔e8** (he can only wait) **41 ♔d3 ♔e7 42 ♔c4 ♖c7 43 ♔d5!** and Black resigned. If 43...♔e8 then 44 ♖a5 and 45 ♖xc5 wins the c-pawn without giving Black the slightest counterplay. White could then advance his queenside pawns and win easily.

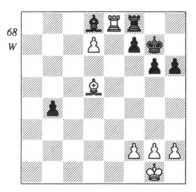

Kramnik – Timman
Novgorod 1995

The shortest example in our book. After **32 ♔f1!** the mere threat of the white king's advance persuaded Timman to resign. White simply puts his king on c8, chasing the bishop from d8, and then queens his d-pawn, winning a piece. Meanwhile Black can do nothing. Note that without the

intervention of the white king, Black's defences would hold.

Black lasted a bit longer in our next game.

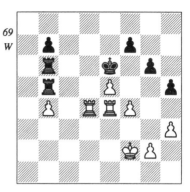

Dolmatov – Sosonko
Cannes 1994

White has an extra pawn, but Black looks solidly entrenched and the white rooks are tied down to b4. Again it takes the intervention of the white king to break the impasse.

38 ♔g3!		**♖d5**
39 ♔h4		**♖c6**

The threat of 40 ♔g5 followed by g4 and f5, breaking through Black's defences, compels Black to give up his passive stance.

40 g4		**hxg4**
41 hxg4		**b5**
42 ♔g5		**♖xd4**

Or 43 f5+ wins the rook.

43 ♖xd4		**♖c4**
44 ♖d6+		

Of course 44 ♖xc4 bxc4 is a draw at best for White. Now Black temporarily regains his pawn, but Dolmatov has calculated that the black kingside will soon be defenceless against White's marauding king.

44 ...	♔e7
45 ♖f6!	

This frees the king from the defence of f4.

45 ...	♖xb4
46 ♔h6!	♔e8

Black is helpless. If 46...♔f8 47 e6 and Black loses all his kingside pawns.

47 ♔g7	g5
48 f5	♖xg4
49 ♖xf7	♖e4
50 e6	

The connected passed pawns easily defeat Black's scattered passed pawns.

50 ...	g4
51 ♔f6	

and Black resigned. If 51...g3 52 ♖g7 ♔f8 53 e7+ ♔e8 54 ♖g8+ ♔d7 55 ♖d8+ and queens.

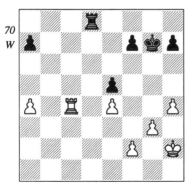

Ribli – Beliavsky
Barcelona 1989

28 ♖c5	♖d4

Giving up the e5-pawn is the best chance, since if 28...♔f6 29 ♖c6+ ♔g7 30 ♖a6! ♖d7 31 ♔h3 and White puts his king on f5, when Black can resign.

29 ♖xe5	♖xa4
30 ♔h3	

The familiar entrance of the white king.

30 ...	a5
31 ♔g4	♖a2
32 f4	a4
33 ♖g5+	♔f8
34 ♖a5	♖a3
35 f5	f6
36 ♖a7	♔g8
37 h5	h6
38 e5!	

White sacrifices a pawn to break Black's blockade on the kingside. Then the combination of his rook on the seventh rank, passed pawn and active king will destroy all resistance.

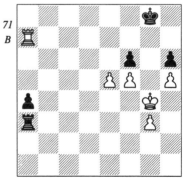

38 ...	fxe5
39 f6	♖b3
40 ♔f5!	a3

If 40...♖xg3 then 41 ♔e6, 42 ♖a8+ and 43 f7 wins.

41 g4

and Black resigned. Either 42 ♔g6 or 42 ♔e6 will be fatal.

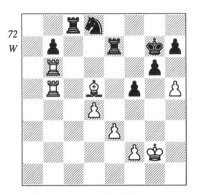

Kasparov – Andersson
Belgrade 1985

White could capture the pawn on b7 directly, but he is loathe to exchange his powerful bishop for the lame black knight after 40 ♗xb7 ♘xb7. Rather than give Black some relief by exchanging, Kasparov prefers to intensify the pressure by bringing up his king.

40 ♔g3! ♖d7

Here 40...gxh5 41 ♔f4 would lose easily.

41 hxg6 hxg6
42 ♔f4! ♖c2
43 ♔g5!

Once again the king is the straw that breaks the back of the defence. Black could defend (just) against the white army, but not against its commander as well.

43 ... ♖xf2

44 ♖xg6+ ♔f8
45 ♗b3!

Uncovering an attack on f5.

45 ... ♘f7+
46 ♔f6! f4

If 46...♖d6+ then 47 ♗e6 with the threats 48 ♖xf5 and 48 ♖a5! intending 49 ♖a8+ ♖d8 50 ♖xd8+ ♘xd8 51 ♖g8 mate (but not 48 ♖xb7?? ♖xe6+ 49 ♔xe6 ♘d8+).

47 e4 ♖b2

Taking on d4 loses the knight.

48 e5 f3
49 e6 f2
50 ♗c4

Black resigned. A possible finish is 50...♖xb5 51 ♗xb5 ♖d6 52 d5 ♖b6 (52...♖xd5 53 e7 mate, or 52...♘d8 53 ♖h6 ♔g8 54 ♔e5 etc.) 53 ♖g7 ♖xb5 54 e7+ ♔e8 55 ♖g8+ and queens.

Our final example of a successful king raid is from the game Psakhis-Hebden, Chicago 1983.

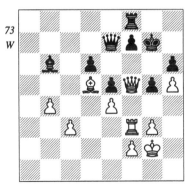

Black is tied down to the f7 pawn. But the opposite coloured bishops and the closed nature of the position make it is difficult to imagine how White will break-through and queen his extra b-pawn. Psakhis shows how it can be done, courtesy of some brave play by the white king.

43	♔f1!	♗a7
44	♔e2	♗b6
45	♔d3	♗a7
46	♔c4	♕c7+
47	♔b3	♕e7

The black queen cannot leave e7 unless it is to give check or mate, as otherwise ♕f6+ would rip up his kingside.

| 48 | g4 | ♗b6 |
| 49 | ♔c4 | ♗a7 |

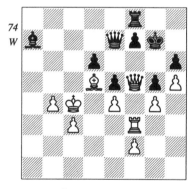

74
W

50 ♔b5!

A bold move made possible by his control over the light squares. If now 50...♖b8+ then 51 ♔a6! ♖b6+ 52 ♔a5 and f7 will drop.

50	...	♕e8+
51	♗c6	♕d8
52	♔c4	♕e7
53	♕d7!	

Now that his king is so well placed, White can swap queens

and then push through the passed pawn.

53...♕e6+ 54 ♕xe6 fxe6 55 ♖xf8 ♔xf8 56 ♔b5 ♔e7 57 ♔a6 ♗xf2 58 c4 ♔d8 59 ♔b7 ♗e1 60 b5 ♗f2 61 b6 ♗d4 62 ♗a4 d5 (desperation) **63 cxd5 exd5 64 exd5 e4 65 ♔c6 ♔c8 66 d6 e3 67 ♗b5 ♗f6 68 ♗a6+ ♔b8 69 ♔d7** Black resigned.

By now the reader probably thinks the king is omnipotent in the endgame and can laugh at any danger. So our final examples are intended as a reminder that even in simplified positions it is possible to be mated.

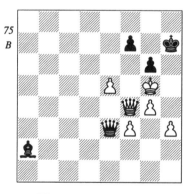

75
B

Fioramonti – Vogt
Switzerland 1995

White is a piece down, but he has two healthy pawns and a grip on the dark squares. Moreover, his king appears to be excellently placed on g5. A shame, then, that he had to resign after **49...f6+!**. There could follow 50 exf6 ♕c5+

51 ♔h4 g5+! 52 ♕xg5 ♕f2+ 53 ♔h5 ♗f7+ winning White's queen.

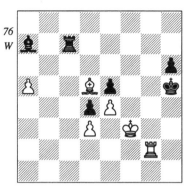

76
W

Skembris – Kuczynski
Moscow 1994

Another illustration of the pitfalls that the king can face even in an apparently simple endgame. Black's last move was **63...♔xh5?** which proved a poisoned feast after

64 ♖g4!

trapping the black king. White now plans to put his king on h3 and then play his bishop to d1, when a subsequent rook to g8 (or somewhere else on the g-file apart from g5 or g6) will be discovered mate.

| 64 | ... | ♗c5 |
| 65 | ♔g3 | ♗b4 |

If Black waits passively then White's plan will be carried out: 65...♗a7 66 a6 ♗c5 67 ♔h3 ♗a7 68 ♖g1 ♗b6 (68...♖c3 69 ♗f7 mate) 69 ♗b3 and 70 ♗d1, mating.

66	a6	♖a7
67	♔h3	♗d2
68	♗c6	

Black resigned. If 68...♖e7 69 a7 ♖xa7 70 ♗e8+ and mate next move.

An active king is a good thing, apart from in the cases when it isn't! So be careful.

4 Exploiting a Material Advantage

"The winning of a pawn among good players of even strength often means the winning of the game". Capablanca.

Before his retirement from chess in the 1850s, Paul Morphy issued an extraordinary challenge to the chess world. He offered all comers the advantage of a pawn and move in a match.

There were no takers. Indeed, Louis Paulsen speculated that the missing pawn could even help Morphy by allowing him to build up an attack along the half-open file.

Nowadays, no World Champion would dare to repeat Morphy's pronouncement. Kasparov would have no chance in a match a pawn down against a front ranking Grandmaster. Indeed, just playing Black in every game (the "move" of Morphy's offer) would make him unlikely to win: we saw in his match with Nigel Short that he was unable to prove any superiority with Black. The reason why pawns and pieces matter so much more these days rests in the enormous advancement of technique. The means of converting extra material into a win, whilst restraining the opponent's counterplay, is in the hands of all strong players. In the present chapter, we aim to share this knowledge with the reader. We begin by looking at a game which is already famous.

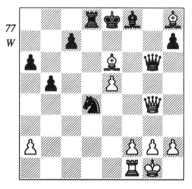

Kasparov – Anand
New York 1995

This is game 10 of the PCA World Championship match. Kasparov had launched a fierce attack involving a rook sacrifice. In order to fend off the assault the Indian Grandmaster had to return the extra rook with a pawn as "interest". However, despite the pawn deficit, things don't seem so bad for Black. White is obliged to swap queens, and after 22 ♕xg6+ hxg6 23 ♗g4 c5 Black has excellent counterplay with his queenside pawns. However, Kasparov found a much better way to exchange queens:

22 ♗f6!   ♗e7

23 ♗xe7 ♕xg4

Black has to exchange queens, because otherwise White gains a winning attack after 23...♔xe7 24 ♕h4+ ♔e8 (24...♔xe6 25 ♕xd8) 25 ♗g4 etc. Since it is Black who exchanges queens, not White, the black h7-pawn isn't transferred to g6 as occurs after 22 ♕xg6+ hxg6. This means that White has connected passed pawns: a crucial strengthening of his chances.

24 ♗xg4 ♔xe7
25 ♖c1!!

A very important move. White has to restrain Black's queenside pawns before advancing on the kingside. A headlong rush with 25 f4 c5 26 f5 c4 27 f6+ ♔f7 28 ♗h5+ ♔e6 would leave the white pawns stymied, while the black c-pawn would be bursting to advance.

Kasparov's move cripples the black queenside counterplay, as it is virtually impossible for him to achieve the ...c5 advance. Now we see another reason why 22 ♗f6 was such a fine move: after 22...♗e7 23 ♗xe7 Black was deprived of the bishop which could have supported ...c5.

25 ... c6
26 f4

Only now. Black has no long-term answer to the advance of the kingside pawns.

26 ... a5
27 ♔f2 a4
28 ♔e3 b4
29 ♗d1!

A further precaution. Kasparov avoids the trap 29 ♖c4 a3 30 ♖xd4 (30 ♖xb4? ♘c2+) 30...♖xd4 31 ♔xd4 b3! and Black wins!

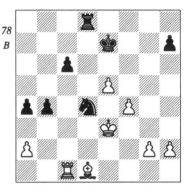

78
B

29 ... a3

If 29...b3 then 30 axb3 axb3 31 ♖b1 wins.

30 g4

The white kingside pawns cautiously edge forwards.

30 ... ♖d5
31 ♖c4 c5
32 ♔e4 ♖d8
33 ♖xc5

Black's gambits the c-pawn for some final tactical tricks.

33 ... ♘e6
34 ♖d5 ♖c8

34...♖xd5 35 ♔xd5 ♘xf4+ 36 ♔c4 ♔e6 37 ♔xb4 ♔xe5 38 ♔xa3 is hopeless for Black, but he might have tried 34...♘c5+!? hoping for 35 ♔d4 b3! However, the simple 35 ♖xc5 wins, e.g. 35...♖xd1 36 ♖c2 ♖b1 37 f5 ♖b2 38 ♔d3 etc.

35 f5 ♖c4+
36 ♔e3 ♘c5
37 g5 ♖c1

38 ℤd6

and after his valiant struggle, Anand finally resigned. Kasparov gives the following plausible finish in *Informator 64*: 38...b3 39 f6+ ♔f8 40 ♗h5 (threatening mate) 40...ℤe1+ 41 ♔f3 (after 41 ♔f2?? ♘e4+ 42 ♔xe1 ♘xd6 Black wins!) 41...♘b7 42 ℤa6 and mate follows.

For his display in this game Kasparov was awarded Best Game Prize for *Informator 64*. No doubt he won this award because of his fine attack earlier in the game (they don't award prizes for endgame technique!). However, without the fine technical moves 22 ♗f6! and 25 ℤc1! he would have failed to clinch victory and all his early brilliance might have been wasted.

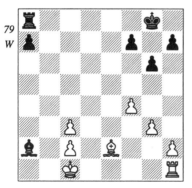

Kasparov – Topalov
Amsterdam 1995

In the above diagram White has three advantages. We can discover the first by counting: White has an extra pawn. Although it is a rather feeble pawn, being both doubled and isolated, other things being equal an extra pawn is almost always worth something.

Secondly, White's king is closer to the scene of action than Black's king: it is better placed either to apprehend the black passed pawn or support his own passed pawn in its advance.

I will have to tell you the third advantage: it is White to move. This allows him to strengthen the position of his king.

25	♔b2	♗e6
26	c4	♔f8
27	ℤa1	a5

The further this pawn advances the weaker it becomes, but if Black leaves it on a7 then White can play ℤa5, ♔c3, ♗f3 and c5, etc. gradually advancing his passed pawn with the support of all his pieces. Topalov realises that this would amount to a slow death and so seeks counterplay.

28 c5!

White doesn't hurry to play 28 ♔c3, since he wants to utilise both his c-pawns.

28	...	♔e7
29	c4	♗d7
30	♗f3	ℤb8+
31	♔c3	a4
32	ℤa3!	

Of course not 32 c6? ℤb3+, but now this move is really threatened.

| 32 | ... | ℤc8 |
| 33 | ♔d4! | |

Better than 33 c6 ♗xc6 34 ♗xc6 ♖xc6 35 ♖xa4. The a4-pawn is very weak and White has no intention of exchanging it for his well supported c5-pawn. Now there is the threat of 34 ♗b7 when, if Black plays 34...♖c7 to deter c6, the manoeuvre ♗a6 and ♗b5 will win the a4-pawn.

33 ...   h5
34 ♗b7!   ♖d8
35 ♔c3   h4

Or 36 c6 wins easily.

36 gxh4!

We may recall Shereshevsky's maxim "do not hurry". Here and on the following two moves White avoids the precipitate c6. First, he forces the black rook to go after the h-pawn and, in its absence, White will find it easier to force through his passed pawn.

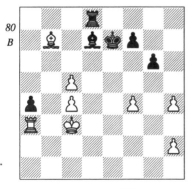

80
B

36 ...   ♖h8
37 ♗d5!

Now White deploys his bishop to its best square rather than shutting it in with c6. The next stage will be to bring up his king to shepherd home the passed pawn.

37 ...   ♖xh4
38 ♔b4

Kasparov wants to vacate the c5 square for his king without permitting Black the blockading ♔d6.

38 ...   ♖xh2
39 c6

Only now.

39 ...   ♗e6
40 ♗xe6!

It wasn't too late to go wrong with the natural 40 ♔c5?, when after 40...♗xd5 41 cxd5 ♖c2+ 42 ♔b6 ♔d6! Black has succeeded in blocking the white pawns. Kasparov's move retains the backward c-pawn, which both shelters the king and protects the forward c-pawn from the attentions of the black rook. Sometimes doubled pawns are more powerful than connected ones!

40 ...   fxe6
41 ♔c5

Kasparov points out a simpler win with 41 ♖d3! cutting off the black king. Then 41...♖b2+ 42 ♔xa4 ♖b6 (the only way to head off the c-pawn) 43 ♖d7+ ♔e8 44 ♖d6 ♔e7 45 c5 etc.

41 ...   ♔d8
42 ♖xa4

and Topalov resigned. Kasparov gives the plausible finish 42...♖f2 43 ♖a8+ ♔c7 44 ♖a7+ ♔c8 45 ♖g7 ♖xf4 (if 45...♖g2, then 46 ♖f7 and 47 ♖f6 wins) 46 ♔b6 and White wins.

Now it is time to see Kasparov's great rival in action.

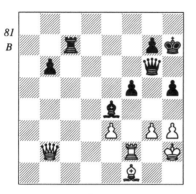

Hertneck – Karpov
Germany 1994

Karpov has a healthy extra pawn, but how is he to exploit it? Conventional wisdom tells us that passed pawns should be pushed but in this case the b5-square is well covered by White's queen and bishop. So Black's winning plan has to be to loosen White's hold on b5. The first stage is to force the exchange of queens with

44 ...   h4!

This forces White's reply, since he cannot allow the break-up of his kingside after 45 gxh4 ♕d6+ 46 ♔g1 ♕g3+ 47 ♗g2 ♗xg2 48 ♖xg2 ♕xe3+.

45 ♕e5   ♖c1!

Do not hurry! Rather than rushing to play 45...hxg3+ Black ties White up further, since 46 ♗b5? ♖h1 or 46 gxh4? ♖xf1 47 ♖xf1 ♕g2 are both mate.

46 ♕f4

White can only wait so by delaying ...hxg3+ Black has gained a tempo to put his rook on a more active square.

46 ...   hxg3+
47 ♕xg3   ♕xg3+
48 ♔xg3   g5!

A very important move which prevents White's king entering the game via f4 for if 49 h4 then 49...g4 gives Black a strong passed pawn.

49 ♗a6   ♖g1+!

Driving back the white king a little bit further before continuing his winning plan.

50 ♔h2   ♖b1!

At last Black has broken the white grip on b5.

51 ♗f1   ♖b3
52 ♗g2   ♔g6!

White is given no chances at all. If 52...♗xg2 53 ♖xg2 ♔g6 54 h4 g4 55 e4! gives White some counterplay.

53 ♗xe4   fxe4
54 ♔g2   b5

Not 54...♖xe3 55 ♖b2! The e3- and b6-pawns are worlds apart in value.

55 ♖c2   ♔h5!

Now 55...♖xe3 is a threat and the horribly passive 56 ♖e2 would allow Black to push the b-pawn all the way to b1, so White defends the e-pawn the other way, but this lets in the black king.

56 ♔f2   ♔h4
57 ♖c5   ♖b2+
58 ♔e1   b4
59 ♔d1   b3

60	Rb5	Kxh3
61	Rxg5	Rg2!

White resigned. If 62 Rb5 b2 followed by taking the e3-pawn with the king, while White can do nothing.

A brilliant example of Karpov's technique. White never had the ghost of a chance.

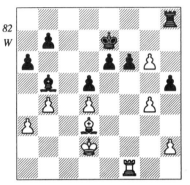

Anand – M.Gurevich
Manila 1990

Anand's play is a perfect illustration of a key principle: allow no chances for the opponent! No "short cut" to the win is to be taken if it gives the opponent the slightest counterplay.

27 g5!

White's first task is to shut the rook on h8 out of the game. Thus, the obvious 27 gxh5 would be a bad blunder, allowing the rook to become active after 27...Rxh5.

27	...	f5

If 27...Bxd3? then White has the winning zwischenzug 28 gxf6+!, whilst 27...fxg5 allows 28 Rf7+

winning quickly after either 28...Kd6 29 g7 Rg8 30 Bh7 or 28...Ke8 29 g7 Rg8 30 Bg6

28	Bxb5	axb5
29	Rc1!	

No chances for Black! White seizes the only open file. The impatient 29 Ke3 allows 29...Rc8 when the black rook can generate some counterplay.

29	...	Kd6
30	Ke3	Rg8
31	Kf4	b6

Black sees that if immediately 31...Rxg6 then 32 Rc8 followed by Rh8 and Rxh5 gives White connected passed pawns, so he waits. However, White has another way to attack h5.

32	Rc3!	Rxg6
33	Rh3	Rg8
34	Rxh5	Rc8

At last the rook becomes active, but Anand has prepared a forced win.

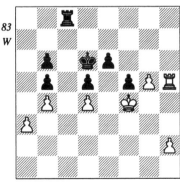

35	g6	Rc4

Too late!

36	Rg5!	Rxd4+

37 ♔e3

Even in a winning position care is needed. It wasn't too late for 37 ♔f3? ♖g4! 38 ♖xg4 fxg4 check! 39 ♔xg4 ♔e7.

37 ...   ♖e4+
38 ♔f2

and Black resigned.

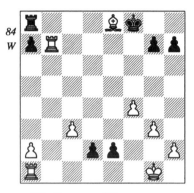

84
W

Hodgson – Masserey
Horgen 1995

White is a rook and a bishop up and has the move. He seems to have a simple win until, of course, you notice the passed pawns on d2 and e2...

28 ♖bb1

The only move.

28 ...   ♖xe8
29 ♔f2   ♖e4!

White has a winning endgame two pawns up after 29...e1♕+ 30 ♖xe1 dxe1♕+ 31 ♖xe1, so Black improves the position of his rook and asks White "what can you do?". Hodgson comes up with a good answer.

30 ♖e1!

This forces Black's hand.

30 ...   dxe1♕+
31 ♖xe1   ♖c4
32 ♖c1!

A superb example of technique. Most club players would automatically play 32 ♖xe2? when after 32...♖xc3 followed by 33...♖a3 it would be very difficult for White to win, if he can win at all.

Instead, Hodgson retains his c-pawn. He correctly judges that the black e-pawn is weak rather than strong, especially since the black king plays no part in the battle.

32 ...   ♖e4
33 ♔e1!

Another accurate move. If 33 c4 then 33...e1♕+! 34 ♖xe1 ♖xc4.

33 ...   h5!

If 33...♔e7 then 34 ♖c2 wins at once: 34...♖e3 is answered by 35 ♖xe2 when 35...♖xc3 is impossible as the rook is pinned. This means that Black's king can never approach the c-pawn. If Black does nothing active, then White can simply push his c-pawn up the board. Hence, Black plans to break-up White's kingside pawns or leave him with a weakness on g3.

34 ♖c2   ♖e3

The only move.

35 c4   h4
36 gxh4!

In *Informator*, Hodgson explains why he avoided 36 c5: 36...hxg3 37 hxg3 ♖xg3 38 c6 (38 ♔xe2) 38...♖g1+ 39 ♔xe2 ♖g2+ 40 ♔d3 ♖xc2 41 ♔xc2 ♔e7 with a draw.

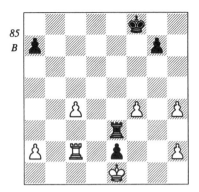

36	...	Rh3
37	c5	Ke7

If, as above, 37...Rxh2 38 c6 Rh1+ 39 Kxe2 Rh2+ 40 Kd3 Rxc2 41 Kxc2 the extra pawn on h4 will win the game.

38	Rxe2+	Kd7
39	Rg2	Kc6
40	Kf2	Kxc5
41	Rxg7	Rxh2+
42	Kg3	Rxa2
43	h5	Ra1
44	h6	Rh1
45	h7	

There was a simple theoretical win with 45 Rxa7 Rxh6 46 Rd7! cutting off the black king from the pawn, but Hodgson's winning method is also straightforward.

45	...	Kd6
46	Rxa7	Ke6
47	Kg4	Kf6

If 47...Rg1+ then 48 Kh5 Rh1+ 49 Kg6 Rg1+ 50 Kh6 Rh1+ 51 Kg7 Rg1+ 52 Kf8 Rh1 53 Kg8 Rg1+ 54 Rg7 and wins.

48 Ra8!

Using a tactical quirk in the position to force the exchange of rooks. This greatly speeds up the win.

48...Rxh7 49 Ra6+ Kf7 50 Ra7+ Kg8 51 Rxh7 Kxh7 52 Kf5 and Black resigned.

In our following example, Black has two extra pawns, but the presence of opposite coloured bishops greatly complicates the winning process.

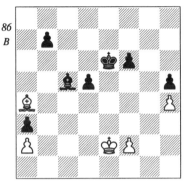

Whiteley – Morris
London 1996

The theme of overstretching the defence by creating widely separated passed pawns is a very important winning endgame technique, and will occur repeatedly in our examination of the present game. As a general rule, in an endgame with opposite-coloured bishops there has to be a gap of at least two files between passed pawns to trouble the defence.

Therefore the following hypothetical position is winning for Black:

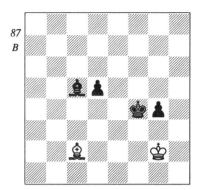

87
B

Black to move plays **1...g3** (not 1...♚e3? 2 ♚g3 and draws) **2 ♗b1 ♗f2** (freeing the king to advance) **3 ♚f1 ♚e3 4 ♗g6 d4 5 ♗f5 d3 6 ♗g6 d2 7 ♗h5 ♚d3 8 ♗d1 ♚c3** and Black's king reaches c1, winning the bishop, or answering ♚e2 with ...g2!

Now we shall see how Black goes about forcing the win in our illustrative game.

41 ...   ♚f5!

White would draw easily after 41...f5 42 ♗e8 ♗e7 43 ♗xh5 ♗xh4 44 ♗e8. He can set up a permanent blockade with his bishop on d3 and his king on f3. Morris describes his winning scheme as follows:

a) Defend the h5-pawn with the king.

b) Attack the h4-pawn with the bishop, forcing White's king to defend it.

c) Get the bishop, b-pawn and d-pawn to their best squares (i.e. the bishop attacking h4, and pawns away from attack by the white bishop)

d) Recentralise the king allowing the h-pawns to be exchanged.

e) Hope Black has enough tempi to force home the passed d-pawn with his king before White's king can return to the centre.

42 ♚f3   ♚g6

It looks paradoxical to retreat the king, but then moves which are part of a well thought out plan can often look strange at first glance. On the other hand, the "obvious" 42...♚e5 should allow White to draw after 43 ♗e8 ♚d4 44 ♗xh5 ♚c3 45 ♗f7 etc.

43 ♗e8+   ♚h6
44 ♗d7   d4
45 ♗b5

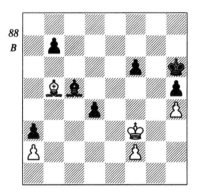

88
B

White could try to stop 45...f5 with 45 ♗f5, but then 45...b5! and 46...b4, and the threat of ...b3 will drag the bishop away from f5.

45 ...   f5
46 ♚g3

After the line 46 ♚f4 ♗e7 47 ♚xf5 ♗xh4 48 f4 ♗e7 the widely spaced passed pawns would win for Black. For example, 49 ♗f1 h4, and if necessary Black will bring his king all the way around the board from h6 to c1 via f8 and c5. White's king could maybe force the win of Black's bishop for the f-pawn, but then the two passed pawns, aided by the black king, would easily overwhelm White's bishop.

46 ...   &e7!

Completing stage b – see note to move 41.

47 &h3?!

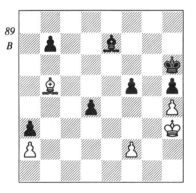

89
B

Here 47 f4! was a better chance. The point is that the black f5-pawn is then a fixed target and the black king is denied the e5-square. These factors will prove important in the game, as we will soon see.

Black can still win after 47 f4, but it is more laborious: 47...&b4 and

a) 48 &d7 &e1+ 49 &h3 d3 50 &xf5 d2 51 &c2 b5 52 &d1 b4 53 &c2 &g7 54 &d1 &f6 55 &c2 &e6 and it's zugzwang: 56 &d1 or 56 &b3+ lose the f-pawn to 56...&f5,

while 56 f5+ &e5 is another zugzwang: White has to hand over either the f5- or h4-pawn.

b) 48 &d3 &e1+ 49 &h3 &g6 50 &c4 &f6 51 &d3 &e6 52 &c4+ &d6 and White can go after either the f-pawn or h-pawn or both, but all to no avail:

b1) 53 &d3 &c5 54 &xf5 b5 55 &g6 b4 56 f5 (56 &xh5 b3 wins) 56...b3 57 f6 &d6! 58 &b1 d3 and wins.

b2) 53 &e2 &c5 54 &xh5 b5 55 &d1 d3 56 h5 &d4 57 h6 &e3 58 h7 &c3 and 59...&d2, winning.

47 ...   f4!
48 &d3   b6
49 &b5   &d8
50 &d3   &g7
51 &e2   &g6!

A notable manoeuvre to ensure that the black king is as far towards the centre as possible before the h5-pawn is given up.

52 &d3+   &f6
53 &g2?

Here 53 &e2 is the last chance, but Black just wins. Morris gives the following analysis: 53...&e5 54 &xh5 d3 55 &d1 &d4 56 &g4 &c3 57 h5 &f6 (care is still required. Black shouldn't rush to queen a pawn or something nasty could happen to him: 57...&d2 58 &b3 &e1 59 &xf4 d2 – 59...&xf2 probably still wins – 60 &f5 &e7 61 h6 &f8 62 h7 &g7 63 &g6 &h8 64 f4 and according to Morris "White's counterplay seems to have won for him") 58 &xf4 &b2! (going after the correct pawn. The white pawns would again be strong after 58...♔d2 59 ♗b3 ♔e1 60 ♔f5 ♗h8 61 f4) 59 ♗b3 (if 59 ♔e3 ♔xa2 60 ♔xd3 ♔b2 wins) 59...d2 60 ♔f5 ♗h8 61 ♔g6 d1♕ 62 ♗xd1 ♔xa2 63 ♗g4 ♔b2 64 ♗e6 b5 65 f4 b4 66 f5 b3 67 f6 ♗xf6 68 ♔xf6 a2 69 h6 a1♕ 70 h7 ♔c2+ 71 ♔f7 ♕h8! wins. Give White just one more tempo – for example if Black plays 71...♕e5?? here – and White draws with 72 ♗xb3+ ♔xb3 73 ♔g8 with a book draw. So after all that effort it could come down to one move! And then all the exclamation marks and question marks I have showered on the text would have to be altered. This would be an analyst's nightmare. So the reader is permitted to discover an easier win for Black in the above analysis, but he mustn't go and find a draw for White!

53	...	♔e5
54	♗g6	♗xh4
55	♗xh5	d3
56	♔f3	♗g5
57	♗e8	♔d4

The black king is now too active.

58	♗a4	♔c3
59	♔e4	

After 59 ♗b3 ♔b2 is zugzwang, for example 60 ♔e4 d2 61 ♔d3 ♔c1 (an instructive blunder would be 61...d1♕+? 62 ♗xd1 ♔xa2 63 ♔c2! slamming the door shut on the black king and so drawing) 62 ♔e2 f3+ and wins.

59	...	d2
60	f3	♔b2

61	♔d3	♔xa2
62	♔c2	d1♕+!

and White resigned. A very tough and instructive game.

Our final example in this section shows what happens when a great player is struggling a pawn down. He calls up enormous powers of resistance and almost saves the game.

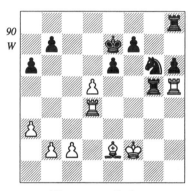

Karpov – Salov
Buenos Aires 1994

White is a pawn down and fighting for his life.

34 ♖b4!

He avoids 34 ♖xg5? hxg5 when the rook on h8 comes to life and instead forces the advance of the black queenside pawns so that they can be broken up.

34 ...   b5

35 a4!

The disappearance of Black's queenside pawns will enhance White's drawing chances. According to Reuben Fine "if you are one pawn ahead, in 99 cases out of 100 the game is drawn if there are pawns on only one side of the board". Fine is right, even if he exaggerated the statistics.

35 ...	♖c8
36 axb5	axb5
37 dxe6	

Continuing his plan of breaking up Black's pawns. Black is also better after 37 c3 ♖xh5 38 ♗xh5 ♖c5!? 39 ♗e2 ♖xd5 40 ♗xb5 (or 40 ♖xb5) though White would have some dynamic chances with his queenside pawns.

| 37 ... | ♖xh5 |

In *Informator 62* Salov points out the drawing defence that Karpov had ready against 37...♖xc2, namely 38 ♖xg5 hxg5 39 exf7! ♘f4 40 ♖xb5 ♖xe2+ 41 ♔f3 ♖g2 42 ♖f5 and the double threat of queening and 42 ♖xf4 secures the draw.

38 ♗xh5	♖xc2+
39 ♔e3	♖c5
40 ♗e2	♖e5+
41 ♔f2	

Here White could force the exchange of rooks with 41 ♖e4. But is it a good idea? The question of when and what to exchange is sometimes highly complex, as we know from chapter 3. In this instance, Karpov declines the opportunity, judging that he has more chances of counterplay if he retains rooks. However, it seems this was an incorrect decision, since the bishop would prove better than a knight on its own.

| 41 ... | fxe6 |

He prefers this to 41...♖xe6. Because he has been denied connected passed pawns, Black now wants pawns as far apart as possible to stretch the white defence.

42 ♗xb5?!

Karpov persists in avoiding the exchange of rooks. But 42 ♖xb5 was in fact better when Black is obliged to exchange.

42 ...	♔f6
43 ♗d3	h5
44 ♖e4	

Now Karpov changes his mind and tries to exchange rooks...

| 44 ... | ♖c5! |

...but the moment has gone. If White persists with 45 ♖c4, then 45...♘e5! A dour phase now begins: Salov seems more intent on torturing his opponent than pressing for the win.

45 ♔e3	♖g5
46 ♔f2	♖f5+
47 ♔e3	♖g5
48 ♔f2	♖f5+
49 ♔e3	

91
B

49	...	♘e7
50	♖h4	♖e5+
51	♔f2	♖d5
52	♗c4	♖f5+
53	♔g1	♖g5+
54	♔f2	♖f5+
55	♔g1	♘g6
56	♖e4	♘f4
57	b4	

At last the b-pawn gets moving.

57	...	♖g5+
58	♔f1?	

After a long, tense fight even the strongest players can collapse. White should play 58 ♔h1! when it is very doubtful if Black can win. The white bishop and rook can defend against the e-pawn, while the king copes with the h-pawn. It's not always correct to centralise the king!

58	...	e5!
59	♗a6	

Already we see the consequences of White's blunder on the previous move. 59 b5 is natural, which leads to a draw with the king on h1, but with the king on f1 Black wins: 59...h4 60 b6 h3 61 b7 h2 and if White queens he is mated in three moves.

59	...	♖g3!

Salov remembers that rooks are best placed behind passed pawns, so he plays his rook to b3 where it is excellently placed both to prevent the white pawn's advance and to support the advance of his own pawns.

60	♖c4	♖b3
61	b5	h4

62	♖c6+	♔g5
63	b6	♖b1+?

There was a simple win with 63...h3 64 ♔g1 (the only defence to 64...h2) 64...♔h4! activating the king, for example 65 b7 ♔g3 and now White loses after either 66 ♖c3+ ♖xc3 67 b8♕ ♖c1+ 68 ♗f1 h2+ and mate next move, or 66 ♖c1 h2+ 67 ♔h1 ♘h3 68 ♖f1 (the only defence to 68...♘f2 mate) 68...♘f2+ 69 ♖xf2 ♔xf2 70 ♔xh2 e4 and the e-pawn will cost the bishop.

64	♔f2	h3
65	♔g3?	

The only defence was 65 b7! h2 66 ♖c1! (Salov), when it is surprising that Black has no forced win. According to Salov, the best line is 66...♖b2+ 67 ♔g3 ♖g2+ 68 ♔f3 ♖g1 69 ♖xg1 hxg1♕ 70 b8♕ ♕d1+ 71 ♔f2 ♕d4+ 72 ♔f1 e4 when Black has a clear advantage.

65	...	♖g1+

Now Black has a simple win.

66	♔h2	♖g2+
67	♔h1	♘h5!

White resigned, as he has to give up his rook to prevent mate by 68...♘g3.

Greater material advantage

A piece up for several pawns

It will be seen from the above examples that when a pawn up, the standard winning plan involves queening, or threatening to queen, a pawn. Perhaps the preparatory stage will involve increasing the positional advantage, forcing the exchange of pieces or capturing more material, but ultimately the way to decide the game is by queening a pawn or forcing the inferior side to give up a lot of material to prevent queening.

With an extra piece or more, the winning method is generally the same as with an extra pawn, but should be much more straightforward. As with a pawn advantage, the main danger is exchanging off pawns too quickly, when the game could burn out into a pawnless endgame with no winning chances.

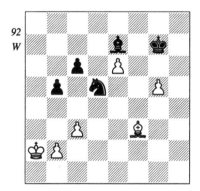

Minasian – Dreev
St Petersburg 1993

White is a piece down and his pawns on e6 and g5 are indefensible. So his only drawing chance is to exchange off both black queenside pawns. This, however, proves impossible.

43 ♔b3   ♔g6

44 c4   bxc4+

The first stage of Black's winning plan is to make sure the c-pawn is inviolable. On c5 it will be safe from capture by the white king or exchange by b4 as long as Black keeps his bishop on e7.

45 ♔xc4   ♘b6+

46 ♔d4   c5+

47 ♔d3

The second stage is to round up the g5- and e6-pawns. For once, the opposite-coloured bishops actually favour the player trying to win. If White had a dark-squares bishop, he would have a chance to liquidate the last black pawn by arranging b4 (although even in this hypothetical situation Black would have winning chances if he managed to prevent b4). As it is, all White can do is wait.

47 ...   ♔xg5

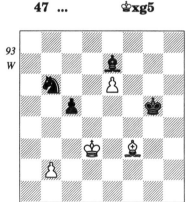

48 b3

The e6-pawn is doomed anyway (Black can attack it with king and knight) so White makes no effort to defend it with his bishop.

48	...	♔f5
49	♗c6	♔xe6
50	♗f3	♔e5
51	♗h5	♘d5

So Black has prevented the exchange of his c-pawn and captured White's loose pawns. Now at last he is ready to exploit his material advantage in an active way. To do so, he needs to queen the c-pawn, or at least force White to give up his bishop to prevent it queening – in this case he will have the theoretical win of bishop and knight against bare king. To queen the c-pawn he first needs to capture the b3-pawn. But how can this be done, since b3 is so well defended? Dreev will show us with his beautiful technique.

The next stage of his plan is to use the combined force of the bishop, knight and king to gradually push White's king backwards. This is achieved by depriving him of squares. It will be seen in what follows that White is unable to contest the control of any dark square, indeed Black is two pieces up on the dark squares.

52	♗f3	♘b4+
53	♔c4	

The white king is evicted from d3, which allows the black king into e3.

53	...	♔f4
54	♗h5	♔e3
55	♔c3	♘c6!

This prepares to take the c4-square away from the white king. Then the bishop will be freed

from defending the c5-pawn and can be used to drive back White's king.

56	♗e8	♘a5!
57	♗f7	♗f6+
58	♔c2	♘c6!

Next move the white king will be deprived of c2.

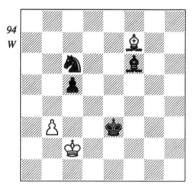

94
W

59	♗g8	♘b4+
60	♔b1	♔d2

Now at last the black king is in sight of its target: the b3-pawn.

61	♗f7	♔c3
62	♗g8	♗g5!
63	♗f7	♘d3!

In order to meet the first threat to the b-pawn, 64...♘c1, the white king is forced forwards to a3.

64	♔a2	♘c1+
65	♔a3	♗e7!

With the threat of 66...c4+ forcing the king another square forwards, when Black wins control of b2.

66	♔a4	♔b2
67	♗c4	♘a2

And now the idea is 68...♘c3+ evicting the white king from a4.

Then Black plays ...♔a3 and ...♘c1 when the b3-pawn is won. White decides to advance his king voluntarily.

68 ♔b5　　♔a3

White resigned. 69...♘c1 follows and the b-pawn is lost.

A fine technical display by Dreev, who is also the hero of our next game.

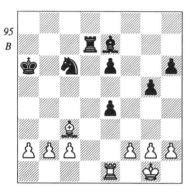

95
B

Akopian – Dreev
Linares 1995

Black's e4-pawn seems doomed and White has three healthy looking queenside passed pawns. Nevertheless, Dreev succeeded in exploiting his extra piece with some forceful play.

31 ...　　♗b4!

A temporary respite for the e-pawn because ♖xe4, here or next move, loses to a back rank mate. White now has the disagreeable choice of allowing his queenside to be shattered by ...♗xc3 or giving up a pawn. Not surprisingly he chooses the latter course.

32 ♗xb4　　♘xb4
33 g3?

Here White should play 33 h4! renewing the threat to the e4-pawn and exchanging off a kingside pawn. As we know, when a piece down the defender should try to exchange off to a pawnless endgame. The move actually chosen does nothing to swap pawns and, even worse, creates a serious weakness in White's pawn structure which Black's pieces can try to exploit.

33 ...　　♘xc2
34 ♖xe4　　♘d4

Now Black is in control since White cannot begin an exchanging strategy: if 35 h4 gxh4 and as 36 ♖xh4? ♘f3+ loses, White has to play 37 gxh4, when his pawns are split and there is no easy way to force further exchanges.

35 ♔g2　　h5!
36 h3

The weakness created by the move 33 g3 plagues White. If 36 h4 g4 37 ♖e5, then 37...♘f3! wins after 38 ♖xe6+ (38 ♖xh5 ♖d1) 38...♔b7 intending 39...♖d1 and mate is unstoppable.

36 ...　　♔b5
37 ♖e5+

A pointless move but White can do nothing constructive.

37 ...　　♖d5
38 ♖e3　　e5
39 ♖c3　　g4
40 hxg4　　hxg4
41 ♖c8　　♘f3
42 ♖g8

Played to meet 42...♖d1 by 43 ♖xg4, destroying the mating net.

42 ...   ♖d4
43 b3

Preventing 43...♔c4, but losing in another way. These are not the most powerful passed pawns you will see in the book! Dynamically speaking, they are almost irrelevant. However, they do serve a defensive purpose: Black is wary of bringing his king to the kingside too quickly, since the pawns could suddenly advance and become dangerous.

43 ...   ♔b4
44 a4   ♖e4
45 ♖g7   ♘e1+!
46 ♔f1   ♘d3

Over the last few moves Black has placed his rook, knight and king on optimal squares. Now he is ready to win of the f2-pawn. Once this pawn drops, Black's e-pawn will become a passed pawn which will decide the game.

47 ♖g6   ♖e1+
48 ♔g2   ♖e2!
49 ♖xg4+

White finds he is unable to defend f2. If 49 ♖f6 then 49...e4 (threat 50...e3) 50 ♔f1 ♖e1+ 51 ♔g2 ♖d1! and 52...♘e1+ is a winning threat, e.g. 52 ♖g6 ♘e1+ 53 ♔f1 ♘f3+ 54 ♔e2 ♖e1 mate.

49 ...   e4
50 ♔g1   ♘xf2
51 ♔f1   ♖a2
52 ♖f4

Has White saved himself? The e4-pawn is pinned and if the

knight moves, then 53 ♖xe4+ draws: White has achieved his aim of eliminating all the pawns.

52 ...   ♔c3!

A pretty winning stroke. If 53 ♖xf2 then 53...♖xf2+ 54 ♔xf2 ♔d2 and the d-pawn queens.

53 a5   e3
54 b4   ♘d3
55 ♖e4   ♔d2

White resigned. 56...♖a1+ and 57...e2 finishes things.

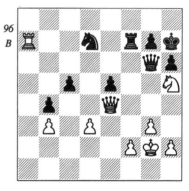

96
B

Salov – Timman
Sanghi Nagar 1994

Here Timman found a brilliant move which won a piece.

43 ...   c4!!

Now 44 ♕xc4? loses directly to 44...♕xh5 45 ♕e6 ♕f3+, whilst 44 bxc4 ♘c5 45 ♕xg6+ ♔xg6 46 ♖a5 (if 46 ♖xf7 ♔xf7 and the b-pawn is unstoppable) 46...♘xd3 is also hopeless for White (Salov).

44 ♕xg6+   ♔xg6
45 dxc4!

The path of maximum resistance. White gives up his knight

in return for connected passed pawns on the queenside.

45	...	♔xh5
46	♖a5	♔g6
47	f3!	

Black cannot save his b-pawn so White takes the chance to rule out ...e4. If immediately 47 ♖b5 then 47...e4! 48 ♖xb4 ♘e5 intending ...♘d3 or ...♖xf2+, and White can resign.

47	...	♔f6
48	♖b5	♖f8
49	♖xb4	♖b8?

The art of exchanging pieces unwisely! Usually every exchange helps when a piece up. However, knights are clumsy versus pawns, especially passed pawns, so here the exchange of rooks lets White hope for a draw: he need only liquidate all the kingside pawns while the black knight and king are engaged in the task of capturing the white queenside pawns.

Therefore, Black should have played 49...♖a8 and ...♖a2+ (Timman) activating the rook, and Black should win.

50	♖xb8	♘xb8
51	b4	♘c6

Black wants to win the passed pawns rather than restrain them. Hence he entices them forwards instead of blocking them with 51...♘a6 52 b5 ♘c5.

52	b5	♘a5
53	c5	♔e6
54	♔f2	♘b3
55	c6	♔d6
56	♔e3	♘d4

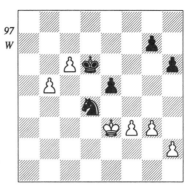

57	b6	♘xc6
58	♔e4?	

A very natural move which, almost unbelievably, is a fatal blunder! After 58 f4! ♔e6 59 fxe5 ♔xe5 it is very doubtful if Black can win. If he goes after the b-pawn with his king then the enemy monarch can eat up his kingside; if he tries to force a zugzwang position on the kingside then the white king can go to the queenside attacking the knight. For example, 60 ♔d3 ♔f5 61 ♔c4 ♔g4 62 ♔c5 ♘b8 63 b7 ♔h3 64 ♔d6 ♔xh2 65 ♔c7 ♘a6+ 66 ♔b6 ♘b8 67 ♔c7 with a draw, or if 60...♔d5 61 ♔e3 ♔c5 62 ♔e4 ♔xb6 63 ♔f5 and if anyone loses it won't be White!

58	...	♔e6
59	b7	

Here is what happens after 59 f4, as given by Salov: 59...♘b8!! 60 fxe5 ♘d7! 61 b7 ♘c5+. The b-pawn is lost and with it all hope for White. Now we can see why 58 ♔e4 was a blunder: the king is separated from b7 by the distance of a knight fork on c5. This allows Black to win the b-pawn if White attempts to liquidate the kingside pawns.

    59 ...   **♘b8**
    60 f4   **♘d7!**
    61 ♔e3

61 fxe5 ♘c5+ wins, or 61 f5+ ♔d6 62 ♔e3 ♔c6 63 ♔e4 ♔xb7 and again White is helpless.

    61 ...   **e4!**
The final artistic touch: Black rules out the exchange fxe5.

    62 ♔d4

Here 62 ♔xe4 is hopeless since after 62...♘c5+ 63 ♔d4 ♘xb7 he cannot exchange off the kingside pawns. 62 g4 also loses, e.g. 62...h5! 63 h3 (63 gxh5 ♔f5 soon wins by zugzwang because Black can play ...♘b8 if necessary) 63...hxg4 64 hxg4 ♔d5 65 ♔e2 (65 f5 ♔e5 or 65 g5 ♔e6 – intending ...♔f5 – and again 66 ♔xe4 ♘c5+ and ...♘xb7 wins) 65...♔d4 66 ♔d2 e3+ 67 ♔e2 ♔e4 68 f5 ♔f4, etc.

    62 ...   **h5**
    63 h3   **♔f5**

    64 ♔e3   **g6**
    65 g4+

65 ♔d4 h4 66 gxh4 ♔xf4 wins, or if 65 h4, then 65...♔e6 66 ♔d4 ♔d6 67 ♔e3 ♔d5 is simplest.

    65 ...   **hxg4**
    66 hxg4+   **♔xg4**
    67 ♔xe4   **♘c5+**
and White resigned. He cannot exchange off the last black pawn.

The exchange up

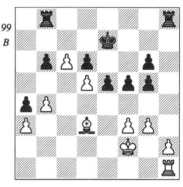

Chandler – Kramnik
Germany 1994

Black is the whole exchange up, but White has a protected passed pawn. So Kramnik began with

    40 ...   **♔d8**
planning to blockade the dangerous pawn with 41...♔c7 and then begin the task of exploiting his material advantage. However, he temporarily leaves his rook on b8 shut off from the kingside and centre. This doesn't seem to be important since the position is closed, and besides it is only for

one move before 41...♔c7 frees it again.

Nevertheless, by striking immediately White could have upset his opponent's hope of a painless victory. With 41 g4! White would break open the position at the worst possible moment for Black's pieces. For example

a) 41...♖f8 42 h4!! prising open the kingside. If now 42...e4, then 43 ♗a6! fxg4? (43...♖h8!) 44 hxg5 gxf3 45 ♖h7 and White wins, or 42...fxg4 43 hxg5 ♖xf3+ 44 ♔e2 threatening 45 ♖h8+ or 45 ♖h7 and White has dangerous play.

b) 41...fxg4 42 fxg4 ♖h3 43 ♗xg6 ♔c7 (43...♖xa3 44 h4) 44 ♔g2 ♖xa3 45 ♖f1! intending 46 ♖f7+ and White has at least a draw.

c) 41...♔c7! 42 gxf5 gxf5 43 ♗xf5 ♖bf8 44 ♗g4 e4 45 ♔g3 exf3 46 ♗xf3 and Black has some advantage.

Whatever the final verdict on 41 g4, it is clear that White's only chance was to do something fast before Black could co-ordinate his more powerful army.

In the game White chose a waiting move and the chance for activity vanished.

41 ♔g2?   ♔c7

Now all danger is passed for Black. He plans ...b5, ...♔b6, the doubling of rooks on the e-file and then ...e4. The passed pawn thus created will break through White's defences.

42 ♖c1

Kramnik recommends 42 b5 stopping Black's next move. Then the black queenside would be less secure than in the game. However, after 42...♖h7 followed by ...♖e7, ...♖be8, ...e4 etc. Black should win.

42	**...**	**b5!**
43	**♖c2**	**♖h7**
44	**♔g1**	**♔b6**
45	**♔g2**	**♖e7**
46	**♖e2**	**♖be8**
47	**♗b1**	**e4**

All according to plan.

48	**fxe4**	**fxe4**
49	**♗a2**	**♖e5**
50	**♔h3**	**e3!**

Now White is virtually in zugzwang: 51 ♖e1 allows ...e2; 51 ♗b1 loses the d-pawn; 51 ♔g4 allows ...♖f8 and ...♖f2, breaking the blockade; and 51 ♔g2, the only other move, could lead to the finish 51...g4 52 ♔g1 ♖f8 53 ♔g2 ♖ef5 54 ♖xe3 ♖f2+ 55 ♔g1 ♖f1+ 56 ♔g2 ♖8f2 mate. White chooses the lesser evil, but its hopeless.

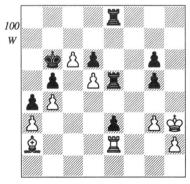

51 ♗b1   ♖xd5

52	♗xg6	♖d2!
53	♖e1	♖e7
54	♗h5	♖h7
55	♔g4	

Loses a piece, but 55 g4 ♖e7 followed by ...e2 and ...♖d1 wins anyway.

55	...	♖d4+
56	♔xg5	♖d5+
57	♔g6	♖hxh5

and White resigned.

Two pieces for a rook

In spite of the limited material available in an endgame, it is sometimes possible to carry out a successful mating attack, but in most cases when the king is in grave danger the threat proves stronger than the execution.

Our final example illustrates this well. A threat of mate completely ties up White's pieces and leaves him defenceless against the standard plan of queening a pawn.

In the following position Black has "only" the material advantage of two minor pieces for a rook. However, these two pieces happen to be a pair of bishops. In the game situation, with lots of open lines, they become a lethal attacking force.

| 22 | ... | ♗f5! |

Activity comes before pawn snatching! After 22...♗xb2 23 ♖b1

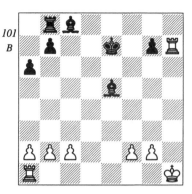

Zapata – Dreev
Wijk aan Zee 1995

followed by 24 ♖h8 Black would be tied up.

23	♖h5	♔f6
24	c3	♗g4
25	♖h4	♔g5
26	g3	

The rook has been crowded out by the black king and bishops; now a weakness is forced in White's kingside.

26	...	♗f3+
27	♔g1	♔f5
28	♖e1	g5
29	♖h7	♗f6!
30	♔f1	♔g6
31	♖h2	

If 31 ♖c7 then 31...♖h8 mates.

| 31 | ... | g4 |

and perhaps out of exasperation, White resigned. His rook on h2 is completely shut out of the game. Black can win as he likes, maybe by ...♖d8 and ...♖d2.

5 Passed pawns and pawn majorities

With the reduction in material which marks the arrival of the endgame, the value of the remaining pieces undergoes change. In the case of the king, it can be a dramatic transformation. In the middlegame his task is one of survival; in the endgame he becomes an aggressive pawn killer. So too with the rook: he is often a passive observer "behind lines" during the early stages of the game, but once most of his foes have vanished he sees his chance to wreak havoc.

For pawns the story is very much the survival of the fittest: strong pawns become stronger, but weak pawns become weaker! Here are two examples.

A far advanced passed pawn, which was firmly restrained in the middlegame, finds it has fewer enemies to block its path in the endgame. Hence it is much more dangerous to the opponent and its restraint may destroy the co-ordination of the enemy pieces.

In contrast, a backward isolated pawn, even if it is a passed pawn, has little dynamic value. Although it could be comfortably defended in the early phases of the game, in the endgame it ties down one of the last remaining pieces to it defence, a great handicap for the defender.

In this chapter we are concerned with a central problem in the endgame: the creation of a passed pawn from a pawn majority and its subsequent queening. From the examples above it will be deduced that both passed pawns and pawn majorities are either weak or strong. They either add value to the player's position or they take something away from it. They can never be defined in neutral terms as "just good enough".

We begin with some examples in which we see the passed pawn as a powerful weapon.

Sudden breakthrough

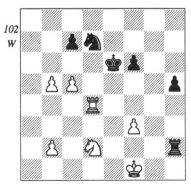

102
W

McDonald – D. Ledger
England 1994

The author remembered that knights are bad against passed pawns and this gave him the idea of

42 b6!

Planning to answer 42...cxb6 with 43 c6 when the black pieces are unable to stop the pawn queening, for example 43...♘e5 44 c7 ♖h1+ 45 ♔g2 ♖c1 46 ♘c4! ♖xc4 47 ♖xc4 and wins.

42 ...	**♖h1+**
43 ♔g2	**♖c1**
44 ♖xd7!	

If now 44...♔xd7 45 b7 and queens. So Black tried

44 ...   cxb6

but soon lost after 45 ♖d6+ ♔e5 46 f4+ ♔xf4 47 cxb6, etc.

In our next game, the wily pawn slips past the enemy knight, king and rook.

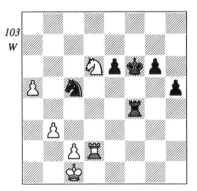

Timman – Kramnik
Horgen 1995

In the above diagram both players have three(!) passed pawns. Although White's most advanced pawn is one step further up the board than Black's, he nevertheless seems worse. Black's pieces are well placed to stop White's pawns rolling (both 42 b4? and 42 c3? lose material) and if White tries the preparatory 42 ♔b2 then 42...h4 43 c3 h3 gives Black the edge. So energetic play is required from White.

42 ♘b7!   ♘xb7

42...♘a6 43 ♖d6 is bad, so he must accept the offer.

43 a6   ♔e7!

If 43...♘c5 or 43...♖b4 then 44 a7 and nothing can stop the pawn, but now it appears that Black will have the advantage after 44 axb7 ♖b4! (but not 44...♖f8? 45 ♖g2! and Black has to give up his g-pawn because 45...♔f6? 46 ♖f2+ loses for him).

44 ♖d8!

Another surprise. Black is forced to block the back rank upon which the pawn runs through.

44 ...   ♘xd8

Or 44...♔xd8 45 a7.

45 a7	**g5**
46 a8♕	

White has won the race to promote. However, Black has enough compensation with his kingside pawns and well co-ordinated rook and knight.

46 ...	**h4**
47 ♕b8	**♘f7**
48 b4	**h3**
49 ♕c7+	**♔f6**
50 ♕c3+	**e5**
51 ♕xh3	

White had to eliminate the dangerous passed pawn, but now Black can play 51...♖xb4, followed by putting his rook on f4 and his knight on c4. Then in view of the impending advance of the black pawns, White would have to force a draw by perpetual check.

Therefore, a draw was agreed after 51 ♕xh3.

Connected passed pawns

An important endgame principle is that connected passed pawns are considerably more powerful than scattered passed pawns. However, this is apparently difficult for computers to grasp, as the following example demonstrates.

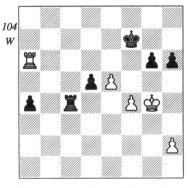

Karpov – Deep Thought
USA 1990

Karpov began with
48 h4!
to rule out 48...g5. Play then continued
48 ...   ♖d4

49 ♖f6+   ♔g7
50 ♖a6   ♔f7
51 h5   gxh5+??

This gives White a pair of connected passed pawns and an easy win. In positions of this type it is the quality, not the quantity, of passed pawns which matters.

Any non-mechanical Grandmaster would automatically (but not like an automaton!) play 51...g5 here, to break up White's pawns at all costs. Black should then hold the draw e.g. 52 ♖xh6 ♖xf4+ (but not 52...gxf4 when 53 ♔f5 looks fatal for Black) 53 ♔xg5 ♖f1 etc. As played, Black's position quickly becomes hopeless.

52 ♔f5!

Of course, he avoids 52 ♔xh5?? ♖xf4: White's f4-pawn and Black's h5-pawn are worlds apart in value. Now the white passed pawns, aided by the king and rook, bludgeon their way through.

52 ...   ♔g7
53 ♖a7+   ♔f8
54 e6   ♖e4

He must stop 55 ♔e5 ♖e4+ 56 ♔d6 forcing the e-pawn through.

55 ♖d7!

A logical continuation. White plans to force the black rook from e4 by destroying its pawn protection. Then, if the rook goes to e1, it no longer attacks f4 and ♔f6 will win; on the other hand, if it goes sideways (e.g. ...♖b4) then ♔e5 and f5-f6 will win.

55 ...   ♖c4
56 ♖xd5   h4

57 ♖d3

Black's remote passed pawns cannot advance while the mutually defending white pawns will power through.

57...♔e7 58 ♖d7+ ♔f8 59 ♖h7 h5 60 ♔e5 h3 61 f5 ♔g8 62 ♖xh5 a3 63 ♖xh3 a2 64 ♖a3 ♖c5+ 65 ♔f6

Black resigned.

Passed pawns supported and unsupported

The most important theme in chess is the co-ordination of the pieces. Therefore, a passed pawn which is helped forwards by an army of pieces is almost always more valuable than a pawn which enjoys no such protection or "encouragement".

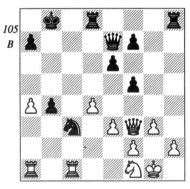

Sosonko – I. Sokolov
Holland 1995

Despite being a pawn down, Black forced the exchange of queens.

26 ...   ♕b7!
27 ♕xb7+   ♔xb7

Now the advanced passed pawn on b4 can be supported by the king as well as the rooks and knight. This means it is far stronger than the white h-pawn.

28 ♔g2   e5!

Black sacrifices a pawn to activate his rooks, while at the same time he prevents the white plan of ♘d2 and ♘b3, when the passed pawn is blocked.

29 dxe5   ♖d3
30 ♖c2   ♖hd8
31 h4!

Reminding Black that White also has a passed pawn.

31 ...   ♔b6
32 e4!

This is an excellent countersacrifice which clears e3 for the knight.

32 ...   fxe4

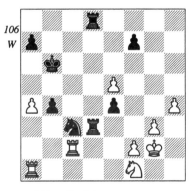

33 a5+??

A disastrous move, which loses an important tempo in a critical situation. In *Informator 64*, Ivan

Sokolov analyses the correct 33 ♘e3! to a draw by repetition after 33...♔c5 34 h5 b3 35 ♖b2 ♔b4 36 ♘c2+ ♔c4 37 ♘a3+ ♔b4 38 ♘c2+ etc. If, after 33 ♘e3, Black plays to win with 33...♖8d4, then 34 h5 b3 35 ♖b2 ♘xa4 36 ♖bb1!? intending 37 h6 is highly obscure.

33 ...   ♔b5

Over the next few moves Black systematically clears away the obstacles in the path of his passed pawn. The king proves an active helper.

34	**h5**	**b3**
35	**♖b2**	**♘a4**
36	**♖e2**	**♖d1**
37	**♖xd1**	**♖xd1**
38	**♘e3**	**♖d8!**

The rook anticipates the advance of the h-pawn.

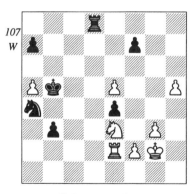

107
W

39	**♘f5**	**b2**
40	**♘d6+**	**♔c6!**

Because the black knight can force through the b-pawn on its own, the king heads towards the h-pawn. Sokolov avoids the trap 40...♖xd6? 41 ♖xb2+! ♘xb2 42

exd6 ♔c6 43 h6, when the h-pawn queens.

41	**♖e1**	**♘c3**
42	**h6**	**♖f8!**

Black could still spoil everything with the impulsive move 42...b1♕ when 43 ♖xb1 ♘xb1 44 ♘xf7 and 45 h7 saves White.

43 g4

If 43 h7 then 43...♖h8. White now makes a good swindling attempt.

43	**...**	**♔d7**
44	**h7**	**♖h8**
45	**♘xe4**	**b1♕**

But not 45...♘xe4 46 ♖b1 ♖xh7 47 ♖xb2, when White has some chances to save the endgame.

46	**♖xb1**	**♘xb1**
47	**f4**	**♔e7**
48	**♘f6**	**♔e6**

Intending ...♘c3 and ...♘d5, exchanging knights or winning the h-pawn.

49	**♘e4**	**♘a3**
50	**a6**	**♘c4**

Planning the sacrifice 51...♘xe5 to force winning simplification.

51	**♘g5+**	**♔e7**
52	**♔g3**	**f6**
53	**exf6+**	**♔xf6**
54	**♔h4**	**♘d6**
55	**♔h5**	**♔g7!**

Preventing 56 ♔h6.

56 f5   ♖b8!

Zugzwang.

57	**f6+**	**♔xf6**
58	**♔h6**	

and here White resigned. After 58...♖h8 it is again zugzwang: 59 ♔h5 ♔g7 or 59...♘f7 wins.

In the next example the white passed pawn was always strongly supported by the king. Black's king, on the other hand, never achieved an active role until it was too late.

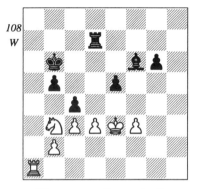

Timman – Ivanchuk
Amsterdam 1994

White found a way to kill off Black's initiative and force a favourable simplification.

34	♖a6+!	♔xa6
35	♘c5+	♔a5
36	♘xd7	♗g5+
37	♔e4	♗c1
38	dxc4	♗xb2

If 38...bxc4 then 39 ♘xe5 wins for example 39...♔b5 (39...♗xb2? 40 ♘xc4+) 40 ♔d4 ♗xb2 41 ♘xg6 followed by 42 ♘e5.

39 c5!

White resists the lure of immediate material gain and instead creates a strong passed pawn. Black would draw easily after 39 cxb5? ♔xb5 40 ♘xe5 ♗xc3 41 ♘xg6 ♔c6.

39	...	♗xc3
40	c6	♔a6
41	♔d5!	

Normally in an open game with passed pawns the player with a bishop has a substantial advantage. However, this position is an exception: the white king, passed pawn and knight are so well co-ordinated that Black cannot even force a draw.

41 ... ♗a5

If 41...♔a7 then 42 ♔d6 b4? (42...♗b4+ giving up e5 is the only chance) 43 c7 ♔b7 44 ♘b6! queens the pawn.

42 ♘c5+!

White keeps control. If 42 ♘xe5 then 42...b4 and Black's passed pawn becomes active enough to ensure a draw.

42	...	♔a7
43	♔d6	♔b8
44	♔d7	

White's king dominates its adversary.

44 ... g5
45 ♘d3!

Again it would be a grave mistake to grasp at material gain. After the continuation 45 ♘a6+ ♔a7 46 c7 ♗xc7 47 ♘xc7 Black can escape with a draw: 47...b4 48 ♘d5 b3 49 ♔d6 b2 50 ♘c3 e4! 51 fxe4 g4 and Black queens first (Timman).

45 ... b4

White always wins the race to queen, for example:

a) 45...♗c7 46 ♘b4 ♗a5 47 ♘d5 (zugzwang) 47...e4 (if 47...♔a7 48

c7 ♗xc7 49 ♔xc7!) 48 fxe4 g4 49
e5 g3 50 ♘e3 b4 51 e6 b3 52 e7.

b) 45...e4 46 fxe4 g4 47 e5 g3
48 ♘f4 ♗c7 49 e6! ♗xf4 50 e7.

46	♘xb4!	e4
47	fxe4	g4
48	♘a6+	♔a7
49	c7	♗xc7
50	♘xc7	g3
51	♘b5+	♔b6
52	♘d4	

and Black resigned. If 52...♔c5
53 ♘f3 g2 (with one more tempo
Black would be able to draw by
queening, followed by ...♔d4) 54
e5 and wins.

The outside passed pawn

We have already seen the great
value of an outside passed pawn
in a pawn endgame (see chapter
1). The lucky possessor of such a
pawn can deflect the opponent's
king from the defence of his main
body of pawns, whereupon his own
king can stroll in and capture all
the undefended pawns.

In the next position we shall examine the same idea in a more
complicated setting.

White has a substantial positional advantage. The e6- and g4-
pawns are both vulnerable and
White's rook controls the only
open file. If Black tries to centralise his king with 34...♔c7, then
White plays 35 c5 chasing away
the knight, followed by 36 ♖f7+.
If 34...c5 then 35 ♖f6 ♖e8 36 ♖g6
wins a pawn.

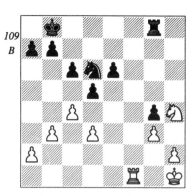

Timman – Lobron
Amsterdam 1994

For this reason Lobron creates
a passed pawn to gain some counterplay.

34 ... dxc4!
35 dxc4

35 bxc4 leaves White with a
weak pawn on d3.

35 ... ♖g5!

A spirited defence. Black rules
out 36 c5 and tries to activate his
rook. In contrast, 35...♖e8 is hopelessly slow after 36 ♖f6 threatening 37 ♖g6.

36 ♖e1!

Timman keeps control of the
position. The careless 36 ♖f6 allows ...♖e5 when Black's rook is
strongly placed.

36 ... e5

Now the black rook has no entry point since even the square f5
is unavailable. Having frustrated
Black's bid for counterplay, Timman now begins his winning attempt.

37 h3!

Timman creates an outside passed pawn. This pawn can be supported by the king which, as we know from the examples above, is an important advantage.

37 ...   **gxh3**

Black could fight for the g4-square with 37...♘f7 38 hxg4? ♘h6 and ...♘xg4, thereby achieving a solid blockade. However, 38 ♖f1! would defeat this plan after 38...♘h6 39 ♖f8+ ♔c7 40 ♖h8 and Black is forced to play the passive ...♘g8.

38 ♔h2   **e4**

If 38...♘f5 then 39 ♖xe5 ♘xh4 40 ♖e8+! (not 40 ♖xg5? ♘f3+) 40...♔c7 41 gxh4 ♖g2+ 42 ♔xh3 ♖xa2 43 h5 and the passed pawn wins the game.

39 ♔xh3   **♔c7**
40 g4   **a5**
41 ♔g3   **♖g8**

Black sees no defence to the white plan of gradually improving his position with 42 ♔f4 and 43 ♘f5, when he will lose his e-pawn. So he sets a crafty trap...

42 c5?!

...into which Timman falls. He should have remembered the principle "do not hurry!" and carried on slowly with 42 ♔f4.

42 ...   **♘e8**
43 ♖xe4   **♘f6**
44 ♖c4   **♖g5**
45 ♘f3

45 ♘f5? ♘xg4 equalises.

45 ...   **♖xc5!**

The point of Lobron's defence: Black regains his pawn. Even so,

the endgame remains dangerous for him.

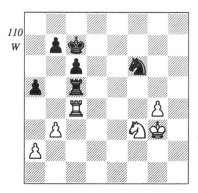

110
W

46 ♖xc5   **♘e4+**
47 ♔f4   **♘xc5**
48 g5   **♔d6**
49 ♔f5   **♘e6?**

Black tries to prevent the advance of the g-pawn with his knight and king, but such an approach is hopeless. As soon as the black king is deflected away from the queenside his pawns become vulnerable to capture.

The only chance of a successful defence was to sacrifice his knight for the g-pawn and eliminate both the white pawns on the queenside. Therefore, the correct initial move was 49...a4! Then play could go 50 b4 (if 50 bxa4 ♘xa4 and now 51 g6 ♔e7 and draws, but 51 ♔f6!? is more promising for White) 50...♘e6 51 g6 ♔e7 52 ♘g5!? ♘xg5 53 ♔xg5 ♔f8 (or else 54 ♔h6 and 55 ♔h7 queens the pawn) 54 ♔f6 a3!? 55 ♔e5 b6 (55...♔g7 54 ♔d6 wins) 56 ♔d6 c5 57 bxc5 bxc5 58 ♔xc5 ♔g7 59 ♔b4 ♔xg6 60 ♔xa3

♔f7 and the black king heads for a8 with a draw.

So it appears Black may just scrape a draw with 49...a4!

50	g6	♔e7
51	♔e5	♘c7
52	♘g5	♘e8
53	♘e6	

The white knight dominates its counterpart.

| 53 | ... | ♘f6 |
| 54 | ♘d8! | |

The decisive breakthrough. Black dare not exchange knights, so he loses his b7-pawn. Such is the power of an outside passed pawn!

54	...	a4
55	♘xb7	axb3
56	axb3	♘d7+
57	♔f5	c5
58	♘d6!	

Now there is a threat of 59 g7 ♘f6 60 ♔g6 ♘g8 61 ♘e4 and 62 ♘xc5.

| 58 | ... | ♘b6 |

and Black resigned before White played 59 g7.

Converting an outside majority into a passed pawn

White has a distinct positional advantage. The b5-pawn is weak, especially because it is on a light square where it can be attacked by White's bishop. The long-range bishop is more valuable than the knight and would become even more powerful if queens were exchanged (the queen and knight

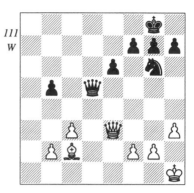

Hübner – Korchnoi
Brussels 1986

are a good force in combination). White's task is to win the b5-pawn or, failing that, to convert his 2-1 queenside majority into a passed pawn.

32 ♕d3

Offering an exchange of queens which Black dare not accept as he then loses his b-pawn.

| 32 | ... | ♕g5! |
| 33 | b4! | |

Fixing the b5-pawn on a light square where it is permanently weak.

| 33 | ... | h6 |

The best chance was 33...♘f4!? offering the h-pawn in return for active play. For example, 34 ♕xh7+ (34 ♕e4 ♘d5 deploys the knight to its best square) 34...♔f8 35 ♕e4 (if 35 ♗e4 ♘e2!? threatening mate) 35...♘xg2! 36 ♕xg2 ♕c1+ regains the piece with a draw. This variation demonstrates the power of the queen and knight as an attacking force.

34 g3!

Black won't get a second chance to play ...♘f4!

34 ...	♛e5
35 ♔g2	f5!?

In the next game we shall eulogise the potential of a central pawn majority when it begins to rumble forwards, but here the advance of Black's pawns isn't well supported and e6 becomes a second target in his position. Nevertheless, it was hard to suggest a constructive plan for Black. Doing nothing was not an option, because White can play ♗d1 and ♗e2, when the b5-pawn is indefensible. Even if Black won the c3-pawn in exchange for his b5-pawn (which is by no means certain), White would get a passed pawn long before Black had mobilised his kingside pawns.

36 ♗b3

Hübner immediately eyes the weakness on e6.

36 ...	♘e7
37 ♛d4	♛e2

If 37...♛xd4 then 38 ♗xe6+ should win after 38...♔f8 39 cxd4 ♘c6 40 ♗xf5.

38 ♗d1

38 ♛d6 is ineffective after 38...♛e4+ 39 ♔h2 ♘d5 and Black defends, therefore White redeploys his bishop to f3 to cover the e4-square. Then his queen will be freed to attack the b5-pawn.

38 ...	♛e1
39 ♗f3	♔f7
40 ♛c5	♔f6

If White ever tries to mobilise his bishop against the b-pawn then he loses control of d5, allowing Black to play ...♘d5 attacking c3. Therefore Hübner decides to give up trying to win b5 and instead creates a passed pawn.

41 c4	bxc4
42 ♛xc4	♛d2
43 b5	♛d6
44 ♛c3+	♔f7

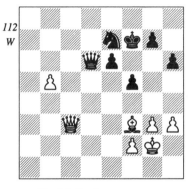

45 ♗h5+!

Accuracy! White provokes a new weakness in the black kingside before continuing with his plan of forcing through the b-pawn. This weakness will prove of decisive importance later on.

45 ...	g6
46 ♗f3	h5
47 ♛e3	♘c8
48 ♗c6	♘e7
49 ♗f3	♘c8
50 h4!	

A sequel to his 33rd move. Hübner fixes the black pawns on light squares where they are vulnerable to attack by the bishop.

50 ...	♕b6
51 ♕e5!	

White waits for a more favourable moment to exchange queens.

51 ...	♘a7
52 ♗e2!	♘c8
53 ♗c4	♘e7

The bishop manoeuvre to c4 ties down the black queen and king to the defence of e6. Black is almost paralysed, since he can only move his knight from e7 to c8 and back again. It is therefore time for White to bring up his king.

54 ♔f3!	♘c8
55 ♔e2	♘e7
56 ♕e3!	

Now that he has improved the position of his king, White offers the exchange of queens.

56 ...	♘d5

Hoping for 57 ♗xd5? ♕xb5+. Black's only chance was 56...♕d6 declining the exchange of queens, but even then 57 b6 should win.

57 ♕xb6	♘xb6
58 ♔d3	♔e7
59 ♔c3	♔d7
60 ♔b4	♔d6
61 ♗a2!	

Zugzwang. If 61...e5 then 62 ♗f7 wins both the g6- and h5-pawns (here we see why White played 45 ♗h5+!), or if 61...♘d5+ then 62 ♗xd5 wins the pawn endgame. Finally, after 61...♔d7 62 ♔c5 the white king breaks the blockade on b6.

61 ...	♘c8
62 ♔a5	♔e5

Of course if 62...♔c7 63 ♗xe6, so the black king cannot oppose the entry of its adversary.

63 f4+	♔d6
64 ♔a6!	e5

Or else 65 b6 wins.

65 ♗f7	

and Black resigned. His kingside will be massacred.

The passed pawn is securely blocked

So far we have looked at examples in which the creation of an outside passed pawn proved very strong. Now we shall look at some positions in which the passed pawn or outside pawn majority proves weak. However, we shall not concern ourselves with positions where the passed pawn can be easily captured.

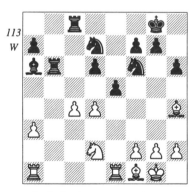

I. Sokolov – Korchnoi
Antwerp 1995

Queens have just been swapped and it appears that Black has

good chances in the coming endgame due to the weakness of the c4-pawn, which can be further attacked with moves such as ...♖bc6 and ...♘b6. However, White's next move leads to a complete transformation of the position.

22	c5!	dxc5
23	dxe5	♗xf1
24	♔xf1	♘d5
25	♘c4	

The weak white pawn on c4 has disappeared and in its place there is a dream square for the knight. Not only is the knight safe from pawn attack here, but over the next few moves White will ensure that Black can never successfully challenge it with ...♘b6. Since the knight is inviolable the passed pawn on c5 is firmly blockaded. White has a clear plan to improve his position by pushing his kingside pawns, while Black can only wait. This is a good example of how a passed pawn, when securely restrained, often proves of less value than the collective might of a pawn majority.

| 25 | ... | ♖a6? |

The only redeeming feature of Black's position is his control of the b-file. Therefore he should have tried 25...♖b3 followed by ...♖cb8, giving his pieces the maximum activity possible.

26 a4!

Sokolov refuses to allow the blockade on the c-pawn to be weakened. Now he is ready to answer 26...♘7b6 with 27 ♘d6 ♖b8

28 a5 ♘d7 29 ♘c4 and the knight returns in triumph, having beaten off the attempt to expel it.

| 26 | ... | ♖b8 |
| 27 | a5 | |

Now Black will never be able to oust the knight with ...♘b6. White can therefore begin his kingside advance.

27	...	♖b4
28	♖ac1	♘c7
29	f4	♘e6
30	♖ed1	♘df8

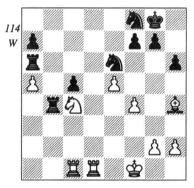

The black knights can only look with envy at their white counterpart on c4. They have no safe squares in the centre, for example if 30...♘d4 then 31 ♗f2 wins. We should point out here that besides White's advantage in pawn structure, he also enjoys the superiority of a bishop over a knight in an open position.

31 ♗e1!

With this move White begins a combination which wins the c5-pawn whilst maintaining an positional control.

31	...	♖a4
32	f5	♘d4
33	g4	h5
34	♘b2!	

The knight is willing to retreat from its dream square if the result is the win of a pawn.

34	...	♖a2
35	♖xc5	♖c6!

The only fighting chance. After 35...♖xb2 36 ♖xd4 Black would have to play 36...♖b8 to avoid being fatally pinned by 37 ♖d8 and 38 ♖cc8. Then White could win another pawn with 37 gxh5, if there was nothing better.

36	♖xc6	♘xc6
37	♘d3	hxg4

White's pawn phalanx proves too strong if Black captures the a-pawn, e.g. 37...♘xa5 38 ♖c1! ♘d7 (to prevent the winning pin 39 ♖c8 and 40 ♗b4; 38...♔h7 is similar) 39 ♖c8+ ♔h7 40 ♖c7 and the white rook eats up a7 and f7 and then the e-pawn marches through.

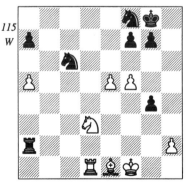

115 W

38	♖c1!	♘e7
39	♗b4	♘d5

Again the rook and bishop prove a fatal combination after 39...♘xf5 40 ♖c8.

40	♖c8	♘xb4
41	♘xb4	♖xa5
42	♘c6	♖b5
43	♔g2!	

A neat final touch. 43 e6?? ♖xf5+ was best avoided, while 43 ♘e7+ ♔h7 44 ♖xf8 ♖xe5 45 ♖xf7 would still have required some effort, but after White's simple king move there is no good answer to the threat of 44 e6 and 45 e7.

Black resigned

The outside majority is blocked

"One unit that holds two"
This is Capablanca's expression to describe one of the key principles of the endgame.

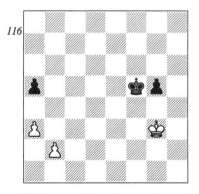

116

White to play draws immediately with 1 b4. However, Black to move can play 1...a4! when he wins easily since the white pawns are paralysed. His winning plan would be simple. First, he drives back the white king with his king and g-pawn. Then, using the g-pawn as a decoy, he switches his king to the queenside, capturing White's pawns and queening the a-pawn. There would also be a simple win by stalemating the white king on g1 and forcing him to play the suicidal b3 (or b4).

In this example the white outside pawn majority proves useless: Black is virtually a pawn up, since his a-pawn is no less valuable than the two white pawns. White cannot convert his majority into an outside passed pawn.

There follows a sophisticated version of this simple idea.

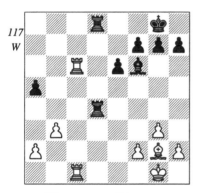

Alterman – Karpov
Tyniste n. Orlici 1995

23 ♖1c2?

White thinks he can draw easily and so selects a passive continuation. Although this should not necessarily lose, it shows that White is only thinking in defensive terms: a suicidal philosophy

against a player who is adept at exploiting small advantages. The best way to defend such positions is to seize the initiative with some healthily active moves. 23 ♖a6! would win the a-pawn. Karpov intended to continue 23...♖d2, when he assesses the position as unclear after 24 ♖xa5 ♗d4. Now if White plays passively he could run into trouble, for example 25 ♖f1 g6 (making a hole for the king and so preparing the following manoeuvre) 26 b4 ♖c8 27 b5 ♖cc2 28 a4 ♗xf2+ 29 ♔h1 ♗d4 and the bishop on g2 dare not move on pain of 30...♖xh2 mate. Therefore 25 ♖a8! is better when after 25...♗xf2+ 26 ♔f1 ♖xa8 27 ♗xa8 g6 28 a4 the game remains balanced: White's kingside is collapsing and Black's pieces are better co-ordinated, but the connected passed pawns are a fearsome sight.

23	...	♖d1+
24	♗f1	g6
25	♔g2	♗e7!

With his uncanny positional sense, Karpov prepares to deploy his bishop to a square where it paralyses White's queenside.

26 ♖c7?

White seems to have lost the thread of the game. Instead of attacking the bishop *en route*, which is pointless, he should make sure that its final destination is not a pleasant one. 26 ♖a6 was better when 26...♗b4 27 a3! dislodges the bishop. Then 27...♗xa3 28

置xa5 is a favourable liquidation for White: the b3-pawn may yet make a name for itself. Perhaps White was still afraid of an attack on his f-pawn, for example by 26...置8d2 27 置xd2 置xd2 28 置xa5 奧f6 when ...奧d4 is unstoppable. However, after 29 a4 奧d4 30 奧c4 置xf2+ 31 含h1 the position remains unclear.

Once again we see that the path to safety for White is to be found in double-edged play. The attempt to draw "solidly" leads to a gradual worsening of White's chances.

26 ...   奧b4

The ideal position for the bishop. White's queenside pawns are now firmly blocked: *they can never advance past the dark-square barrier created by the mutually defending a5-pawn and bishop*. Thus, White's two queenside pawns are worth no more than Black's one pawn on a5. This means that from the point of view of strategic planning, Black is a pawn up. Karpov now has a clear plan to strengthen his position: a gradual advance of the kingside pawns, exploiting his extra pawn there.

Meanwhile all White can do is mark time and wait for his opponent's attack. Such a prospectless position is very difficult to defend against Karpov.

27 置c8

A sure sign that White is floundering. If he wanted to play this

way then he should have done so on the previous move. In any case, it was better to keep both pairs of rooks on the board, since it would prove more difficult for Black to bring up his king, which is a vital part of his winning strategy.

27 ...   置xc8
28 置xc8+   含g7

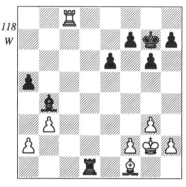

29 置c2   含f6
30 奧e2?

Consistently passive. The one weak point in Black's position is f7, so White should have taken the chance to activate his rook with 30 置c7!, then

a) 30...奧e1 31 奧b5 置d2 32 含f1! 奧xf2 33 奧e8 and White draws easily.

b) 30...置d2 31 a4 followed by 32 奧c4 or 32 奧b5 and it is doubtful if Black can make any progress.

30 ...   置d7!

Denying White's rook the seventh rank.

31 h4   e5
32 h5?

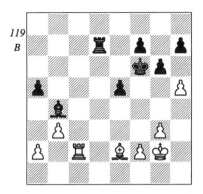

As a general rule it favours the defender to exchange as many pawns as possible, but here White cedes the g5-square which proves an excellent post for Black's king. White should have played 32 ℤc6+ driving the black king back, and only then h5. Alternatively, he should have avoided the pawn advance altogether. Then Black would find it hard to advance his kingside pawns without his king being harassed by White's rook. Note that in spite of the obvious progress Black has made, White would still draw fairly comfortably if he could force the exchange of rooks.

32 ...   ♚g5!

Here the king is safe from attack and can support the advance of the kingside pawns.

33 hxg6   hxg6
34 ♚f1   ℤd6
35 ♚g2   f5
36 ♚f1   ♚f6
37 ♚g2

Karpov suggests 37 f3 here. The drawbacks to this move are obvious: it weakens the kingside pawns and the king's cover. On the other hand, White gains some space and Black cannot subject him to the bind he achieves in the game. Furthermore, if Black subsequently advances ...e4, then White can exchange pawns, and it would be hard for Black's passed pawn to break through the e2-barrier.

Instead White passively awaits his fate.

37 ...   e4
38 ♚f1   ♚e5
39 ♚g2   g5

With every move Black gains more space.

40 ♚f1   ℤh6
41 ♚g2   ℤd6
42 ♚f1   ℤd8

He wants the white king to be on g2 and so waits a move.

43 ♚g2   f4!

The gradual advance of Black's kingside majority produces its first direct threat.

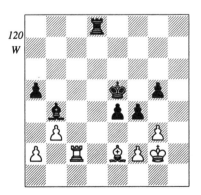

44 f3

A major concession, but otherwise 44...f3 will strangle his kingside. For example, if 44 ♔g1 then 44...f3 45 ♗f1 ♖d1 46 ♖b2 (what else?) 46...♗d2! 47 ♖c2 e3 and wins. The exchange 44 gxf4+ also doesn't help because 44...gxf4 45 f3 e3 is similar to the game, except that Black has the extra option of a breakthrough on the kingside.

44 ...   e3
45 g4   ♖d2!

A player trying to win has to be very cautious about entering an opposite-coloured bishop endgame since there are all sorts of drawing resources available to the defender. Sometimes even a big material or positional advantage can prove worthless. However, in this instance Karpov has correctly calculated that the passed pawn he creates on d2 will win the game. Even so, some subtle play is required to avoid the draw, as will be seen.

46 ♖xd2   exd2
47 ♗d1   ♔d4

Now that the rooks have been exchanged the black king is free to march in along the dark squares.

48 ♔f2   ♔c3
49 ♔e2   ♔b2
50 ♔d3   ♔b1!

An accurate finish. 50...♔xa2? would be a bad mistake, when White draws by 51 ♔c2! shutting in the enemy monarch. The only way for the black king to escape from the corner would be 51...♔a3

and 52...a4, but after 53 bxa4 the queenside pawns would be exchanged and Black's only passed pawn on d2 would be heavily blockaded.

The line 50...♔c1 51 ♔e2 ♗e7 is also insufficient to win, when White draws by 52 b4! ♗xb4 53 ♗b3. Again, Black only has one passed pawn which is solidly blockaded and the white a2-pawn is secure from capture. Karpov realises that he needs to create a second passed pawn if he is to break White's blockade, therefore he puts White in zugzwang and obliges him to give up both his queenside pawns.

51 a3

If 51 a4 ♔b2! 52 ♔e2 (or 52 ♗e2) 52...♔c1 and wins.

51 ...   ♔c1!
52 ♔e2

Both 52 ♗e2 ♗xa3 and 52 axb4 ♔xd1 lose at once.

52 ...   ♗xa3

Zugzwang again.

53 b4   axb4

If White still had his a2-pawn he would draw with 54 ♗b3 etc. That is why it was so important for Karpov to force its capture with 51...♔b1! Now White has no defence to the second passed pawn. Black has only to put his bishop on e3 and free his king to force through the b-pawn.

54 ♗a4 ♗b2 55 ♗d1 ♗d4 56 ♗b3 ♗e3 57 ♗a4 ♔b2 58 ♔d1 b3 59 ♗c6 ♔a1

and White resigned.

In the next example, Black's central majority is again triumphant. The white queenside majority is too passive for too long.

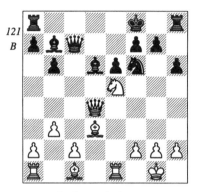

Leko – Adams
Dortmund 1996

17 ...　　　Wc5!
Black forces the exchange of queens so that his king will be secure and well placed in the centre.
18 ♗b2
White cannot refuse as 18 Wb2 ♘e4!? looks bad for him.
18	...	Wxd4
19	♗xd4	♖d8
20	♗b2	♔e7
21	♖ad1	♗c5
22	♔f1?	

After 22 c4, fighting for control of d5, chances remain equal. It would then be reasonable to predict a double exchange of rooks along the d-file and a quick draw.
22 ...　　　♘d5!
23 a3
23 ♗e4? ♘e3+! 24 fxe3 ♗xe4 would be bad for White, but 23 g3

looks better. Then 23...♘b4 24 a3 ♘xd3 25 ♘xd3, attacking g7 and intending ♘xc5, is OK. As played, White is forced to weaken his kingside.
23 ...　　　♘f4!
24 f3?!
Here 24 g3!? was the lesser evil. The game move leaves a target on f3 and also exposes the king to danger because of Black's control of the c5-g1 diagonal.
24	...	f6
25	♘g6+	♘xg6
26	♗xg6	a5!

Beginning a policy of restraining White's queenside majority. The immediate idea is 27...♗a6+ 28 c4 (28 ♗d3 ♗xd3+ leaves White with an isolated pawn) 28...a4! shattering the pawn structure. Here we see that the white king is very badly placed on f1.
27 ♗d3
White prevents the above-mentioned threat, but now that g6 is vacated Black's kingside pawns are free to advance.
27 ...　　　g5
28 ♗c4
28 ♗e2 was probably a better way of defence, planning to offer a double exchange of rooks along the d-file.
| 28 | ... | e5 |
| 29 | ♗c1 | h5?? |

Black's kingside pawns become dangerous. There is now the threat of ...g4 and if White replies fxg4, Black acquires a protected passed e-pawn, while if White allows

...g4xf3 he will be left with a weak pawn. Meanwhile White's queenside majority does nothing. Nevertheless, we should recommend the alternative 29...♖xd1 here, as tactics come before strategy...

30 ♗e3??

This loses control of the open file, but things were already very difficult for White, unless, that is, he plays 30 ♖xe5+! fxe5 31 ♗xg5+ with an instant win. It seems that the strategic nature of the fight has blunted the tactical awareness of both Adams and Leko and, it must be admitted, the author. John Nunn spotted 30 ♖xe5+! when shown the manuscript.

30 ... ♗xe3

Of course if 30...♖xd1 then 31 ♗xc5+. After the mutual blindness on the previous move, the game resumes its normal course.

31 ♖xd8 ♖xd8
32 ♖xe3 ♖d1+
33 ♖e1 ♖d2!

This forces the white rook to e2 (if 34 ♗d3, then 34...g4 is strong) where it obstructs the defence ♗e2 after a subsequent ...g4 by Black.

34 ♖e2 ♖d4!

Naturally Black avoids the exchange of his strong rook.

35 ♔f2 g4
36 ♗d3 h4

Intending 37...h3!

37 fxg4

Finally White concedes a passed pawn to Black. Maybe 37 ♗e4 was a better try, when Black should

avoid easing White's game with a bishop exchange. Instead, he can keep the tension with 37...♗c8 or win a pawn with the variation 37...♗a6 38 c4 a4 39 bxa4 gxf3 40 gxf3 ♖xc4 41 ♖b2 ♖xa4 42 ♖xb6 ♖xa3; however, in this latter line White's active pieces give him drawing chances.

37 ... ♖f4+!
38 ♔g1 ♖xg4

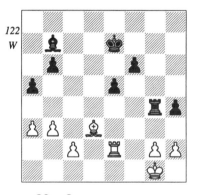

39 c3

At last a sign of activity from White's queenside pawns, but Black has a huge head start in a pawn race.

39 ... ♗d5!

Black wants to advance ...f5, so he plans to put his king on e6 without being bothered by the reply ♗c4+.

40 b4 ♔e6
41 ♖f2 ♖g5
42 c4 ♗c6
43 ♗f1 axb4
44 axb4 f5
45 ♖a2 f4
46 ♖a6

Finally the white rook has become active and with the demise of b6-pawn the queenside majority will become dangerous, but it has all taken too long. In the meantime Black has prepared a winning blow on the kingside.

46	...	♗xg2!
47	♖xb6+	♔f5
48	♖b8	

If 48 ♗xg2, then 48...h3 wins. White is hampered in the pawn race by the dreadful position of his king.

48	...	h3
49	c5	e4
50	♖f8+	♔e5
51	c6	e3
52	♗xg2	

52 c7 ♗e4+ forces mate.

| 52 | ... | ♖xg2+ |
| 53 | ♔f1 | ♖c2! |

As usual a rook is best posted behind a passed pawn. White is now defenceless against the entry of Black's king and as we already know, passed pawns supported by the king almost always beat unsupported ones.

54	b5	♔e4!
55	♔e1	♔f3
56	♔d1	♖c5
57	♖e8	♔f2

White resigned as there is no defence to the threat of ...f3 and ...e2+. A fine display by Michael Adams, who clearly knows all about passed pawns!

6 Breakthrough in minor piece endgames

Many years ago at a junior tournament I happened to play against the World's Dullest player. One by one he exchanged the pieces off until there only remained a blocked pawn centre and one knight each. Then he smugly offered a draw. In reply, I recall looking at his row of pawns (which were intertwined with mine) then looking at my knight, and then reluctantly shaking hands with him. Draw!

It is clear that at the time I had no conception of strategic planning. Otherwise, instead of looking at his pawns and wondering how I could capture them with my knight, I would have gazed at the **gaps** between his pawns and worked out how my king or knight could infiltrate through them. I still have the scoresheet of this game. At the time I thought his pawn centre was an impregnable barrier; now I realise it was full of holes.

The purpose of this chapter is to help the reader improve not only his handling of minor piece endings but also his ability to form plans in blocked positions of all types. In such cases, playing 'move by move' is useless: a well-formulated plan is essential.

The importance of a hole

This concept will be best understood by examining the diagram below.

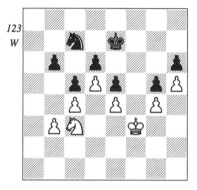

Kasparov – Hübner
Hamburg 1985

White's whole strategy is built around the gap in Black's pawn structure on f5. To White this is a beautiful outpost square; to Black it is a horrific hole. Kasparov intends to put his knight on f5 when the d6- and h6-pawns will become very vulnerable, and then threaten to break through on the queenside with his king. When zugzwang is thrown in as well, Black's defences will be overstretched, as will be seen.

41 ♘d1!   ♘e8

There is no time for 41...b5 since after 42 ♘e3 and 43 ♘f5 White wins a pawn.

42 ♘e3   ♘g7

Just in time to keep the knight out.

43 ♔e2

After 43 ♘f5+? ♘xf5 44 exf5 White can never win since if his king wanders to a4, the black passed pawn on e5 would begin advancing. Now he begins the second stage of his plan. The king plans to break into Black's position via a4 and b5.

43 ...   ♔d7
44 ♔d3   ♔c7
45 ♔c2   ♔c8
46 b4!

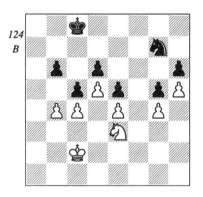

124
B

This plans the exchange bxc5, when, after the recapture ...bxc5, the a5-square is cleared for the white king.

46 ...   ♔c7

If 46...cxb4 then 47 ♔b3 regains the pawn. After the move played Black can only dream that White will reply 47 b5?? when

there is no entry point for his king and a draw can be agreed.

47 ♔b3   ♔b7
48 ♔a4   ♔b8

Here we see the value of White's space advantage. Black would like to play 48...♔a6, blocking the approach of the white king. But then 49 ♘f5! wins: 49...♘xf5 (or he loses a pawn) 50 gxf5 g4 (the black king is too far away to stop the f-pawn) 51 f6 g3 52 f7 g2 53 f8♕ g1♕ 54 ♕a8 mate.

It follows that the black king cannot go beyond the b-file if he wants to stop the f-pawn created after ♘f5 and so he is unable to prevent the white king edging its way into his position.

49 bxc5   bxc5
50 ♔a5   ♔b7

Now 50...♔a7 is natural, maintaining the opposition and keeping out the white king, but once again 51 ♘f5 forces the win for example 51...♘xf5 52 gxf5 g4 53 f6 g3 54 f7 g2 55 f8♕ g1♕ 56 ♕e7+ ♔a8 (56...♔b8 57 ♕xd6+) 57 ♕d8+ ♔b7 58 ♕b6+ ♔a8 59 ♕a6+ ♔b8 60 ♕xd6+ etc.

51 ♔b5   ♔c7
52 ♔a6   ♔c8
53 ♔b6   ♔d7
54 ♔b7   ♘e8

Desperation. If 54...♔e7 55 ♔c6 is zugzwang.

55 ♘f5 ♘f6 56 ♘xh6 ♘xe4 57 ♘f5 ♘f6 58 h6 e4 59 ♔b6 ♘h7 60 ♔b5

and Black resigned. The knight on f5 is still dominant: it ties down the black king to d6 and prevents the advance of the passed e-pawn. Meanwhile, the black knight has to keep watch over the h-pawn, so Black can do nothing at all active. This means that White can simply move his king back to e2 and then continue ♘g3 and ♘xe4, winning the e-pawn because if Black answers ...♘xe4, then h7 queens.

Creating a hole

In the above game the key to White's victory was exploiting the hole on f5, which allowed him to break into Black's otherwise solid position. It is a good idea to inflict such a weakness or weaknesses on the opponent whenever possible, since it will facilitate a later breakthrough.

In the following game Kasparov has the unfamiliar role of victim.

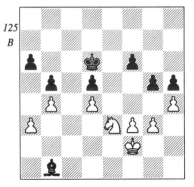

125
B

The diagram is taken from game nine of the first world championship match between the two great champions. As in the previous example, White has a small advantage because in this fixed position his knight is more useful than the bishop. Still, after, for example, 46...♗g6 it is difficult to see how White can win.

But Kasparov thought it was simpler to play

46 ...   gxh4

first, planning to meet 47 gxh4 by 47...♗g6 creating a blockade. However, Karpov responded with the astonishing move

47 ♘g2!!

After 47 gxh4 White would only have one entry point on the kingside. He could put his king on f4, but then what? Karpov temporarily sacrifices a pawn to give himself **two** entry points, on f4 and h4. This means that Black is unable to set up a perfect blockade.

47 ...   hxg3+

If 47...h3 48 ♘f4 wins both h-pawns.

48 ♔xg3   ♔e6

Kasparov gives back the extra pawn straight away in order to bring up his king. After 48...♗g6 49 ♘f4 ♗f7 50 ♔h4 ♔e7 51 ♘xh5 all pawn endgames are lost for Black, for example 51...♗xh5 52 ♔xh5 ♔f7 53 ♔h6 (zugzwang) 53...♔e7 54 ♔g6 ♔e6 55 f4 ♔e7 56 f5 etc.

49 ♘f4+   ♔f5
50 ♘xh5!

The correct capture. Black would have escaped after 50 ♘xd5

♔g5 (threat 51...h4+) 51 f4+ ♔f5, but now there is the threat of ♘g7-e8-c7, picking up the a6-pawn. In order to prevent this, Black's king has to retreat.

50	...	♔e6
51	♘f4+	♔d6
52	♔g4	♗c2
53	♔h5	♗d1
54	♔g6	♔e7

If 54...♗xf3 then 55 ♔xf6 and White wins in three stages: ma-noeuvre his knight to f7 or f5, driving back the black king, then play ♔e5 and finally capture the d-pawn with ♘e7+ and ♘xd5. Kasparov hopes to avoid this slow death by activating his king.

55 ♘xd5+ ♔e6

This loses the a-pawn while the f-pawn remains doomed. Slightly better was 55...♔d6 but then 56 ♘c3 ♗xf3 57 ♔xf6 would be agony for Black.

56	♘c7+	♔d7
57	♘xa6	♗xf3
58	♔xf6	♔d6
59	♔f5	♔d5
60	♔f4!	

The attack on the bishop gains a vital move to defend the d4-pawn, otherwise it would be a draw. Commenting on this game for BBC Television, Hartston re-marked here "this move shows that Karpov is either extremely good or extremely lucky".

60	...	♗h1
61	♔e3	♔c4
62	♘c5	♗c6
63	♘d3	♗g2

64 ♘e5+ ♔c3

If he plays 64...♔b3, then 65 ♔d3 ♔xa3 66 ♔c3 and White forces through the d-pawn, begin-ning with ♘g6, ♘f4 followed by d5.

65 ♘g6 ♔c4 66 ♘e7 ♗b7 67 ♘f5 ♗g2 68 ♘d6+ ♔b3 69 ♘xb5 ♔a4 70 ♘d6 Black resigned.

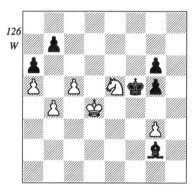

Jagupov – Muhametov
Javoronki 1995

It seems as though all the entry squares have been denied to the white king, but he found a classic breakthrough method.

62	b5!	axb5
63	c6!	bxc6
64	♔c5!	

Now c5 is a huge hole in Black's queenside. White's last move pre-vents ...c5 and highlights the weakness of the bishop in such positions. If 64...♔xe5, then 65 a6 and the pawn is unstoppable.

64	...	b4
65	a6	b3
66	♘c4!	

The knight, on the other hand, has no difficulty in stopping the black passed pawn.

66	...	♗f1
67	a7	♗xc4
68	a8♕	b2
69	♕b7	

Black resigned. If 69...♗b5 then 70 ♕f7+ and 71 ♕b3 stops the b-pawn.

Opening the position to prove the superiority of bishop over knight

The bishop thrives on open lines but finds itself obstructed in blocked positions. Therefore, in a battle between bishop and knight, the question of whether the position remains closed or becomes open is of vital importance.

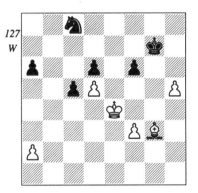

McDonald – P. Littlewood
London League 1996

White has a clear advantage: an outside passed pawn and a strong bishop against a feeble knight.

But how is he to break through and win? The obvious move is 40 ♔f5, but after 40...♔f7! no progress is possible since 41 h6? is inadvisable: 41...♘e7+ 42 ♔e4 f5+ 43 ♔d3 (43 ♔f4 ♔g6!) 43...♘xd5 44 ♗xd6 ♘b4+ and 45...♘xa2, drawing.

White had a long time to contemplate what to play next, because the game was adjourned in the diagram position. To be honest I went home thinking I was winning easily, but the position contained complexities I had failed to see. Originally I had intended to play 40 ♗f4. Then the following moves are more or less forced: 40...♔f7 41 ♗h2 (waiting) 41...♔g7 42 h6+ ♔xh6 43 ♔f5 (White has given up his passed pawn to force his way through Black's barricade) 43...♔g7 44 ♔e6 c4 (the only chance for counterplay) 45 ♔d7 ♘b6+ 46 ♔xd6 c3 47 ♗f4 c2 48 ♔c6 (48 ♔e6 ♔f8! holds the draw).

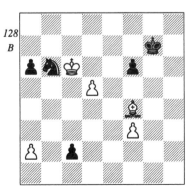

No-one would blame Black for resigning here: his own passed

pawn is stymied while White's will cost him a piece. A classic demonstration of the superiority of the bishop over the knight, or so it seems. In fact, the knight produces a miracle and saves the day: 48...♘c4 49 d6 ♘e5+ 50 ♔c7 ♘xf3! 51 d7 ♘g5!!

An incredible knight's tour, especially as knights are supposed to be bad against passed pawns! If now 52 d8♕, then 52...♘e6+ 53 ♔c8 ♘xd8 54 ♔xd8 ♔g6 looks like a draw with best play. The best chance for White is 52 d8♘! with a peculiar material balance. White probably has a small advantage, but that is all.

White could try to improve on this line with an immediate 40 a5, to rule out ...♘b6 later on, but after 40...a5! 41 ♗e1 ♘b6 42 ♗xa5 ♘xa4 43 ♔d3 (best) 43...♘b2+ 44 ♔c3 ♘d1+! 45 ♔d2 ♘b2 46 ♗c7 ♘c4+ 47 ♔d3 ♘e5+ 48 ♔e4 ♘f7 49 ♔f5 c4 Black has counterplay. The exchange of a-pawns has eased his defence.

In fact, after seeing 51...♘g5 I became dissatisfied with the whole variation beginning with 40 ♗f4. When the game resumed, I chose

40 h6+

Littlewood was relieved when I played this move, as he had thought he was completely lost after 40 ♗f4 etc.

40 ...   ♔g6!

Keeping up the blockade. If 40...♔xh6 41 ♔f5 ♔g7 42 ♔e6 c4 43 ♗e1! stopping the passed pawn

before it crosses the third rank. Then the white king wins the d-pawn with ♔d7 and this time there are no tricks.

41 h7   f5+!
42 ♔f4   ♘e7!

If 42...♘b6 then 43 h8♘+! (better than allowing 43...♘xd5 mate) 43...♔f6 44 ♗h4+ ♔g7 45 ♔xf5 ♔xh8 46 ♔e6, winning.

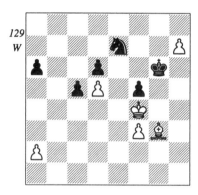

43 h8♘+!

Not 43 h8♕ ♘xd5 mate. Here my opponent shook his head in mock disappointment.

43 ...   ♔g7
44 ♔g5

At last the white king breaks into Black's fortress, and the superiority of the bishop over the knight gives him good winning chances.

44 ...   ♔xh8
45 ♗xd6   ♘xd5
46 ♗xc5   ♔g7

If Black could sacrifice his knight for the white f-pawn and get his king to a8, he would draw, as White has the "wrong" rook's pawn. Hence he moves his king up immediately and makes no effort to defend the f5-pawn, which is lost sooner or later.

However, after the game it was established that 46...f4! would make the win more difficult for White. For example, 47 ♗d6 ♔g8 (47...♘c3? 48 ♗e5+) 48 ♗xf4? (White should play 48 ♔f5 first) 48...♘c3 49 a3 ♘b5 50 a4 (50 ♗c1!) 50...♘d4 51 ♔g4 ♔f7 52 ♗d2 ♘xf3! 53 ♔xf3 ♔e6 etc. and draws through reaching a8.

47	♔xf5	♔f7
48	♔e5	♘c3
49	a3	♔e8
50	♔d6	a5

White will soon win the a-pawn as well. However, things still remain tricky since the black king reaches the a-file. This means he can secure the draw by giving up his knight for the f-pawn.

51	♔c6	a4
52	♗d4	♘e2
53	♗e3	♘g3
54	♔b5	♘f5
55	♗f2!	

The bishop dominates the knight and prevents it from attacking the f-pawn.

55	...	♘d6+
56	♔xa4	♔d7
57	♔b4	♔c6
58	a4	♘f7
59	f4	

Black threatened 59...♘e5 60 f4 ♘d3+ so the pawn takes another cautious step forwards.

| 59 | ... | ♘d6 |

60	a5	♔b7
61	♗c5	♘f5
62	♔b5	♘g3
63	a6+	♔a8

The black king has been forced to a very passive square, so White decides that it is time to bring his own king over to help force through the f-pawn.

64	♔c6	♘f5
65	♔d5	♔b8
66	♔e4	♘g7
67	♔e5	♔a8
68	♗d4!	

An immediate 68 ♔e4 allows 68...♘h5 69 f5 ♘g3+ 70 ♔e5 ♘xf5.

| 68 | ... | ♔b8 |
| 69 | ♔e4 | |

If now 69...♘h5, then 70 ♗e5+! ♔a7 71 f5 ♔xa6 72 ♔f3 and 73 ♔g4, winning the trapped knight, so the knight's blockade of f5 collapses.

69	...	♘e6
70	f5	♘g5+
71	♔d5	♔c7
72	♗e3	♘f7
73	♔e6	♘d8+
74	♔e7	♘c6+
75	♔e8	♔c8
76	f6	♘e5
77	♗f4	

The knight is finally defeated by the combined efforts of the bishop and king.

| 77 | ... | ♘c4 |
| 78 | a7 | |

Black resigned. His last hope was 78 f7 ♘d6+!? 79 ♗xd6? with stalemate. But even on the last move White can win by ignoring the knight: 79 ♔e7 ♘xf7 80 ♔xf7 (zugzwang!) 80...♔d7 81 a7.

In the next example, Karpov shows excellent technique in a minor piece endgame. However, we shall join the game at an earlier stage to show how he begins the winning process. It is too good to miss!

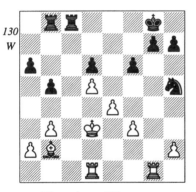

Karpov – Illescas
Dos Hermanas 1994

White has the better pawn structure, the better king and the better minor piece. Karpov's aim is to achieve the better rooks, when his advantage will become decisive. His plan centres on using the c6-square, a bad hole in Black's position, as an outpost for a rook. If White plays ♖c6 and Black replies ...♖xc6, then dxc6 will give White a strong passed pawn; if Black ignores the rook on c6, then White can double rooks along the c-file with total domination.

The obvious way to begin this plan is 25 ♖c1, but Karpov is in no hurry and first creates another weakness in Black's pawn structure.

25 ♗a3!

This forces Black either to give up control of the c-file with 25...♖d8, which is total surrender, or to play the game move.

25 ...   b4

Now the b-pawn is weak and the c4-square becomes Black's second hole on the c-file. This square is a potential entry point for the white king to attack Black's queenside after the exchange of rooks.

26	♗b2	♔f7
27	♖c1	♘f4+
28	♔e3	g5

This weakens Black's pawn structure further and leaves a target on f6, but on the plus side it maintains the knight on its active square, which is a hole in White's position: White can never oust the knight with a pawn. Knights love safe, central positions, so we do not criticise this move. Black's problem is that White has too many positional advantages on the queenside.

29	♗d4	♔e7
30	♖c6!	

This converts the advantage of the c6 outpost into a passed pawn.

30 ...   ♖xc6

Black has no real choice, as otherwise 31 ♖gc1 would be killing.

31	dxc6	♖c8
32	♖c1	♘e6

33 &b6

Keeping control. In *Informator 60*, Karpov shows that 33 ♖c4? is too impatient: 33...♘c5! 34 &xc5 dxc5 35 ♖xc5 ♔d6 36 ♖f5 ♔e6, drawing.

33 ... ♘c5
34 c7 ♘e6

Or 34...♔d7 35 ♔d4 ♘e6+ 36 ♔d5 ♘xc7+ 37 ♖xc7+ ♖xc7 38 &xc7 ♔xc7 39 ♔e6 and White wins (Karpov).

35 ♖c4!

Here we see the value of 25 &a3, which provoked 25...b4. If there were no hole on c4, White's strategy would falter against the threat of 35...♔d7.

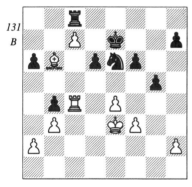

131
B

35 ... ♔d7
36 ♖xb4 ♘xc7
37 ♖c4!

White wants a bishop v. knight ending rather than a rook ending after 37 &xc7? Now the threat to enter a winning pawn endgame compels Black to exchange rooks. Then White's multiple advantages – queenside majority, weak

black pawns and strong bishop – guarantee the win.

37 ... ♘e8
38 ♖xc8 ♔xc8
39 ♔d4 ♔b7
40 &a5 ♔c6
41 ♔c4 ♔d7

If 41...♘c7, then 42 &xc7 gives an easily won pawn endgame, whilst 41...♘g7 42 &c3 ♘e8 43 &d4, followed by gradually advancing the queenside pawns, wins as in the game.

42 &c3 h5
43 a4 ♔e6
44 &d4

The most accurate. If 44 b4 then 44...♘c7 45 b5 axb5 46 axb5 d5+! gives Black some counterplay (Karpov).

44 ... f5
45 exf5+ ♔xf5
46 ♔d5! ♔f4
47 b4 ♔xf3
48 ♔c6!

A position which illustrates the superiority of the bishop over the knight when it comes to a race between pawns on opposite wings. Should the black pawns on the kingside ever become dangerous, White can always sacrifice his bishop to eliminate the last remaining pawn. Black, on the other hand, cannot sacrifice his knight to eliminate White's queenside pawns.

Try a little experiment. Remove the white bishop from the board and replace it with a white knight. Do the same with Black's knight:

replace it with a black bishop. Suddenly you will see that Black has good chances. Admittedly, the position would then be one of the oddest ever seen in chess: both kings would be in check!

48	...	g4
49	b5	axb5
50	a5!	

White wants to queen his a-pawn, since there is an important discovered check.

| 50 | ... | ♔e4 |

After 50...h4 51 a6 g3 52 a7 gxh2 53 a8♕ h1♕ 54 ♔d7+! White wins the black queen.

51 a6

Black resigned.

The knight proves superior to the bishop

We have already seen two examples in which the knight defeated the bishop in the section on creating a hole (see above). Notably, there was Karpov's marvellous 47 ♘g2!! move against Kasparov. In general, it can be said that the knight thrives in blocked positions, with just a couple of free squares in the interlocked pawn structure which can serve as entry points.

Preferably, these free squares (the 'holes' of our earlier section) should be on opposite-coloured squares to the opponent's bishop.

A position doesn't need to have an interlocked pawn structure to be definable as "closed", as the next example shows. In spite of the open lines, the pawn structure meant that the position was closed enough to deprive the bishop of any activity.

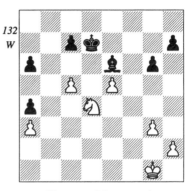

Short – Motwani
Isle of Lewis 1995

White's knight on d4 and his pawns on c5 and e5 are beautifully co-ordinated: they form an absolute barrier which the black king can never break through. The black bishop controls two open diagonals, but it cannot attack anything. Here we see the main weakness of the bishop in comparison to the knight: it can only operate on squares of one colour. If you slide the bishop from e6 onto e7, a dark square, then White would have to work out how to hold the draw.

However, Black's plight may be blamed on his bad pawn structure just as much as the bishop. If his a6-pawn were on b5 instead and it were Black to move, then he could play 35...b4! 36 axb4 a3 37 ♔f2(?) a2 38 ♘c2 ♔c6 39 ♔e3 ♗f5 40 ♘a1 ♔b5 followed by 41...♔xb4 and Black wins. Then we would be extolling the advantages of the bishop over the knight! When talking about "good" knights and "bad" bishops, it is important to keep the overall situation on the board in mind. In the game the black pawn was of course on a6, and he had no queenside play. Short won in effortless style by bringing up his king.

35 ♔f2 ♗d5
36 ♔e3 ♔e7
37 ♔f4 h6

He has to prevent 38 ♔g5 and 39 ♔h6. Now White uses his h-pawn to ram the defences and force a way through.

38 h4 ♗a2

If 38...♔f7 then 39 h5! gxh5 40 ♔f5 followed by e6, ♔e5 and ♘f5(+) wins.

39 ♔e4 ♗b3

Here 39...♔f7 was better, so that 40 h5 gxh5 41 ♔f5 can be met by 41...♗b1+, keeping out the king. Then Short would have had to find a slower winning method, perhaps with g4 and h5.

40 h5!

A typical breakthrough.

40 ... ♔f7

After 40...gxh5 41 ♔f5 there is no longer an option of checking the white king, as 41...♗c2+ loses the bishop. Therefore the blockade begins to crumble.

41 e6+ ♔f6

42 hxg6 ♗a2

Or 42...♔xg6 43 ♔e5 etc., as in the game. White also wins easily after 42...♗xe6 43 ♘xe6 ♔xe6 44 g7 ♔f7 45 g8♕+ ♔xg8 46 ♔d5 ♔g7 47 ♔c6.

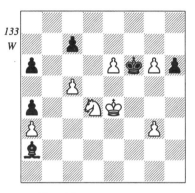

133
W

43 g7!

Another familiar motif. Black's king is deflected from its control of e5.

43 ... ♔xg7
44 ♔e5 ♗b3
45 ♘f5+ ♔g6
46 ♘d6!

A pleasing finishing touch. He threatens 47 e7, and if 46...cxd6+, then 47 cxd6 and 48 d7 will queen.

Positional draw

It was stated above that a knight prefers a blocked position with just a couple of open squares. If there are no open squares at all, then the position is hopelessly , blocked and there is no advantage in having either knight or bishop.

Bent Larsen uses the expression "shop shutting" to describe the process of making a position so blocked that neither side can hope to win. The following is a good example.

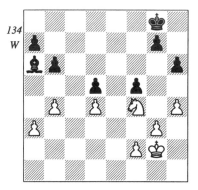

McDonald – Hoogendoorn
Tilburg 1996

White has the advantage because of Black's bad bishop (assuming, of course, that he avoids 35 ♘xd5? ♗b7 when the bishop ceases to be bad and the knight ceases to exist!).

35 ♔f3

White could set Black some serious problems with the less than obvious 35 ♘g6! This threatens 36 ♘e7+ and 37 ♘xf5. Play could continue 35...♔f7 36 ♘e5+ ♔e6 37 ♘c6 ♔d7 38 ♘xa7. Now if Black tries to win the knight immediately he loses after 38...♔c7? 39 b5 ♗b7 40 h5! ♔b8 41 ♘c6+ ♗xc6 42 bxc6 ♔c7 43 ♔f3 ♔xc6 44 ♔f4 ♔b5 45 ♔xf5 ♔c4 46 ♔e5. For example, 46...b5 47 f4 ♔b3 48 g4 ♔xa3 49 g5 hxg5 (49...b4 is similar: 50 gxh6 gxh6 51 f5 b3 52 f6 b2 53 f7 b1♕ 54 f8♕+ ♔a2 55 ♕a8+ ♔b2 56 ♕b8+) 50 fxg5 b4 51 h6 gxh6 52 gxh6 b3 53 h7 b2 54 h8♕ b1♕ 55 ♕a8+ ♔b2 56 ♕b8+ and White exchanges queens followed by ♔xd5, winning the pawn endgame.

So Black has to ignore the trapped knight for a move and ensure that the white king cannot break through on the kingside. This is achieved with 38...g5! e.g. 39 hxg5 hxg5 and White cannot win after 40 b5 ♗b7 41 f4 g4 42 ♔f2 ♔c7 43 ♔e3 ♔b8 44 ♘c6+ ♗xc6 45 bxc6 ♔c7. One possible line runs 46 ♔d3 ♔xc6 47 ♔c3 (or 47 a4 b5! and now White would even lose after 48 a5? b4 49 ♔c2 ♔b5 or 48 axb5+? ♔xb5 49 ♔c3 ♔a4 50 ♔d3 ♔b4 51 ♔d2 ♔c4 52 ♔e3 ♔c3 etc, but the precise 48 ♔c3! bxa4 49 ♔b4 a3 50 ♔xa3 ♔b5 51 ♔b3 still draws) 47...♔b5 48 ♔b3 ♔a5 49 a4 b5 50 axb5 ♔xb5 with a draw.

As the game proceeds Black succeeds in establishing a total blockade.

35	...	♔f7
36	♔e3	♗c4
37	♘g2	♔f6
38	♘e1	g5
39	♘f3	♗b5
40	hxg5+	hxg5
41	♘d2	♔e6
42	f4	g4
43	♘b1	♗d7
44	♘c3	b5!

A paradoxical move, making the bad bishop feel even worse. But never mind, there is no way for the white king to break into Black's position.

45 ♘e2 ♔d6 46 ♘c1 ♔c6 47 ♔d3 ♔b6 48 ♔c3 a6 49 ♘d3 ♗c8 50 ♔b3 ♔c6 51 ♘c5 ♔b6 52 ♘xa6!

and White offered a draw which it would be hard to refuse. White would only lose after 52...♔xa6 if he accidentally touched his a-pawn.

Of course, shop shutting is an extreme form of positional draw. The next position is a more typical example in which White could have established a positional draw if he had found the correct way to maintain a blockade.

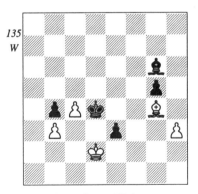

Kamsky – Shirov
Buenos Aires 1994

Black's more active king and far advanced passed pawn (he has just played 54...e3+) give him the initiative. Even so, the protected passed pawn on c4 is a strong asset for White and should save him from defeat.

55 ♔e1?

An instructive blunder. White thinks his king's task is to blockade the passed pawn, but he had a much more important, if less obvious, duty, namely to prevent the black bishop attacking his b-pawn. 55 ♔d1! was correct and Black cannot win, e.g.

a) 55...♗e4 56 ♗d7 ♔e5 57 ♗g4 ♔f4 58 ♗d7 and there is no way for Black to progress (analysis by Shirov in *Informator 62*). The white passed pawn on c4 is always ready to advance if Black's king wanders too far away. Similarly, an exchange of bishops will draw since the pawn on c4 saves White.

b) 55...♔c3 56 c5 ♗e4 57 ♗d7! ♔xb3 58 c6 and it is Black who must work out how he can force a draw.

Therefore, 55 ♔d1! would have led to a positional draw. Instead White loses.

55 ...   ♗c2!
56 ♗d1

Forced.

56 ...   ♗e4
57 ♗g4   ♔c3!

Compare this with note b at move 55 and it will be seen that White is a tempo down: the black bishop is already on e4. This is of crucial significance, because if 58 ♗d7 then 58...♔xb3 59 c5 ♔a3 60 c6 b3 61 c7 b2 62 c8♕ b1♕+ (here the tempo Black has won is obviously a matter of victory or defeat) 63 ♔e2 ♕d3+ 64 ♔e1 ♕d2+ 65 ♔f1 ♕f2 mate.

58 ♔e2

Alternatively 58 ♗d1 ♗g2 59 ♔e2 ♔d4! and wins the h-pawn (Shirov).

58 ...   ♔xb3
59 ♔xe3   ♗g2
60 ♗e6

The excellent position of the bishop on g2 means that White cannot save the game e.g. 60 c5 ♔a3 and wins.

60 ...   ♔c3
61 ♔f2

After 61 c5 ♗c6! White is in zugzwang, for example 62 ♗f7 ♗d7 wins the h3-pawn, 62 ♔f2 ♔d4 wins the c-pawn and 62 ♗g4 b3 sets about queening the b-pawn (Shirov).

61...♗c6 62 c5 ♔d4 63 ♔g3 ♔xc5 64 ♔g4 ♗d5 65 ♗f5 b3 66 ♔xg5 ♔d4 67 h4 ♗e4 68 ♗e6 b2 69 ♗a2 ♔c3!

We have already seen this winning technique in our essential knowledge section.

70 ♔f4 ♗h7 71 h5 ♔b4 72 h6 ♔a3 and White resigned.

Manoeuvring for a breakthrough

In the following games we see the themes discussed above applied in high-class strategic battles. In every case White attempts a breakthrough while Black tries to maintain a blockade.

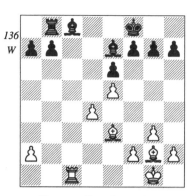

Kramnik – Lautier
Horgen 1995

White has control of the c-file, but it appears that there is nothing to prevent Black unwinding his game with ...♔e8, ...♔d8, ...♗d7, ...b6 and ...♖c8, when he achieves equality. Kramnik, however, has other ideas.

19 ♗h3!!

A brilliant move. White pins the e6-pawn against the bishop on c8, so that he can advance his d-pawn and turn it into a protected passed pawn. In his notes in *Informator 65*, Kramnik points out the false trail 19 d5 exd5 20 ♗xd5 ♗e6 21 ♗xe6 fxe6 22 ♖c7 b5 23 ♖xa7 (23 ♗xa7 ♖a8 paralyses the bishop as retreat allows ...♖xa2) 23...b4 and with the inevitable exchange of the last queenside pawns after ...b3, a draw becomes the most likely result (though Black would still suffer).

Kramnik's actual move keeps a big advantage in a more complicated setting.

19 ...   ♔e8

Instead, 19...f5 (of course if 19...♗d7, then 20 d5) would be dangerous, e.g. 20 exf6 ♗xf6 21 d5 when 21...♔f7 22 ♖xc8! and 21...♔e7 22 ♗c5+ ♔f7 23 ♗d6 ♖a8 24 ♖xc8 both win for White.

20 d5   ♗d7
21 d6   ♗d8
22 ♗g2

Its mission accomplished, the bishop returns to its strong diagonal. Now White intends 23 ♗xa7 ♖a8 24 ♗e3 ♖xa2 25 ♗xb7, winning a pawn. Black has to concede a hole on c6 in order to defend his queenside.

22 ...   b6
23 f4   ♖c8
24 ♔f2   ♖xc1
25 ♗xc1   ♗b5
26 ♗e4!

Forcing a weakness in Black's kingside.

26 ...   h6

This does the least damage. The alternative 26...g6 weakens f6.

27 ♗e3

Now White prevents the advance of Black's b-pawn.

27 ...   ♔d7
28 ♔e1   ♗c6
29 ♗d3!

It is important to avoid the exchange of bishops, as will be seen.

29 ...   ♗d5
30 a3   f6

Lautier tries to give his d8-bishop some breathing space with ...fxe5. The drawback is that the e6-pawn is weakened.

31 ♔d2   fxe5
32 fxe5   ♔c6
33 ♔c3!

After some preparatory moves, Kramnik decides it is time to formulate a winning plan.

It is clear that White has a considerable advantage due to his passed pawn and the sorry state of Black's bishop on d8. In the centre, this bishop is denied freedom by White's d6- and e5-pawns, while on the kingside the only move is ...♗g5, which leaves Black with weak pawns after ♗xg5 hxg5. The queenside is similarly inhospitable: his own pawn on b6 gets in the way, and moving the queenside pawns makes them vulnerable to White's rampant bishops. Thus the bishop must remain entombed for many moves, perhaps forever. How is White to exploit this to win?

He needs to achieve one of three set-ups:

Scenario 1

Black to move: zugzwang.

This could occur after White plays ♗b5+ and Black responds ...♗c6. White then plays a4, or if he has already played this move, he plays a waiting move. Now Black to move is in zugzwang. After 1...♗g5 2 ♗xg5 hxg5 3 g4 g6 4 h3 is still zugzwang, while 1...♗xb5 2 ♔xb5 allows White to win with 3 ♔a6.

Note that this winning scheme fails if White plays ♗xc6+? himself, since after ...♔xc6 no breakthrough is possible: the white king is kept out of b5. That is why at move 29 it was important for White to avoid the exchange of bishops with 29 ♗d3.

Scenario 2

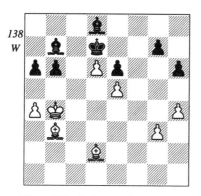

Here Black has adopted a defensive formation with ...♗b7 and ...a6, trying to keep the queenside blocked. Notice that White has played the useful move h4, denying the bishop on d8 the g5-square. Now White can destroy the blockade with 1 a5! Then 1...bxa5+ 2 ♔c5 is decisive, e.g.

2...♗c6? 3 ♗xe6+ alternatively 2...♗a8 3 ♗a4+ ♔c8 4 ♗e8 ♗b7 5 d7+ ♔b8 (forced) 6 ♔d6 and White wins.

If, after 1 a5!, Black tries to keep it closed with 1...b5 he loses by zugzwang: 2 ♗e3 g5 3 h5 ♗f3 4 ♗b6! (threat 5 ♗xd8 and 6 ♗xe6) 4...♗xb6 (4...♗g4 5 ♔c5) 5 axb6 ♗b7 (5...♗xh5? 6 b7) 6 ♔a5 ♗c8 7 ♗d1 ♗b7 8 ♗g4! with zugzwang: 8...♗c8 9 ♗f3 or 8...♗d5 9 ♗xa6 or 8...♔d8 9 ♗xe6.

Scenario 3

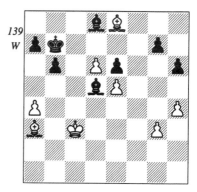

White achieves this set-up in the game. Black has responded to ♗b5+, not with ...♗c6 (when we have the scenario one above) but by moving his king away to b7. Now White wins the black kingside pawns with d7 and ♗f8.

White has to aim for one of these three set-ups. How it is done is revealed by Kramnik's exemplary play.

33	...	♗f3
34	♗c4	♗d5
35	♗a6	♗f3

If 35...♔d7 36 ♗b5+ ♗c6 37 ♔b4 we reach the scenario 1 above. White wins because zugzwang will compel Black to play ...♗xb5, allowing ♔xb5, ♔a6 and ♔xa7.

36 ♔d4   ♗d5

Kramnik set the trap 36...b5? 37 ♔d3 ♗b6 38 ♗xb6 ♔xb6 (winning the bishop?) 39 ♗xb5!

37 a4   ♗b3?

White's last move contained a threat which Black overlooks. He had to try 37...♔d7. Then after 38 ♗b5+, the continuation 38...♗c6? 39 ♔c4 a6 40 ♗xa6 ♗xa4 41 ♗b5+ ♗xb5+ 42 ♔xb5 wins for White. However, Black can fight on with 38...♔c8! (Kramnik). Now 39 ♗c4? ♗xc4 40 ♔xc4 ♔b7! 41 ♔b5 a6+ 42 ♔c4 ♔c6 defends satisfactorily by keeping the white king out, so White would probably carry out a plan similar to that in the game (scenario three above): ♗d2, ♗b4, d7+, and ♗f8, attacking the kingside pawns. If Black succeeds in defending the pawns by advancing them, then they will become weak, and an inroad for White's king would appear.

38 ♗b5+   ♔b7
39 ♗d7!

Now the black king is cut off from d7 and consequently cannot help defend the e6-pawn or prevent the advance of the d-pawn. This means that scenario three can be implemented (see note at move 33).

39 ...   ♗d5

40 ♔c3   ♗a2
41 ♔b4?!

Kramnik points out that he should have played 41 h4 first...

41 ...   ♗d5?

...since Black could have gained space on the kingside with 41...g5!, making White's plan less effective. Lautier doesn't seem to have noticed Kramnik's intention and waits.

42 h4!

Black has missed his chance. If he ever tries ...g5 now, White can respond h5, when the h6-pawn is left weak (and Black can never attack h5 with ...♗f3 because of ♗xe6).

42 ...   ♗a2
43 ♗d2!

A finesse. He wants to time his moves so that the black bishop is on a2, rather than d5, at move 46.

43 ...   ♗d5
44 ♗c1   ♗a2
45 ♔c3   ♗d5
46 ♗a3   ♗a2
47 ♗e8

Now we see why he delayed a move with 43 ♗d2. If the black bishop were on d5 here then 47...♗c6! would be a defence (48 ♗f7 ♗d7). If Black had left his bishop on d5 and tried moving his king instead for example 46...♔b8 last move, it wouldn't have helped since after 47 ♗e8 ♗c6 would simply have lost a piece.

47	...	♗d5
48	d7	♗c6
49	♗f8	

Scenario three has come to pass!

49	...	♗xa4
50	♗xg7	♔c7
51	♗xh6	♗xd7
52	♗f7	

Kramnik has calculated that there is no good way for Black to stop the h-pawn. The rest is simple:
52...♔c6 53 h5 ♔d5 54 ♗g7 ♗g5 55 g4 ♔e4 56 h6 ♗xh6 57 ♗xh6 ♔xe5 58 g5 ♔f5 59 g6 ♔f6 60 ♗g5+ ♔g7 61 ♔d4 ♗a4 62 ♔e5 ♗c2 63 ♗f6+ ♔f8 64 ♔f4

Black resigned.
The simplest way to win is to move the king to h6 and then play ♗e5 and ♗d6+.

It has been stated that, assuming everything else is equal, in blocked positions the knight is normally more valuable than the bishop. Suppose, however, that the possessor of the bishop has important positional or material advantages. Does the inferiority of the bishop stop him pressing home his advantage? An important question, which is examined in the next two games.

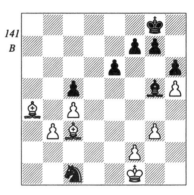

Salov – Karpov
Buenos Aires 1994

Here Black should play 40...♘a2, restraining the b3-pawn. Instead he chose

40	...	♗f6?

This exchange makes positional sense. Karpov wants to eliminate Salov's dark-squared bishop, leaving him with the feeble looking bishop on a4. Then he can put his knight on b4, strangling White's queenside pawn majority, and advance his king. Black could then torture White with the theme of "one unit holding two" discussed in chapter 5.

The plan is fine, but Karpov has overlooked a tactical point.

41	♗xf6	gxf6
42	b4!	

Salov forcibly demolishes the blockade before it can be bolstered with 42...♘a2. The superiority of the bishop over the knight in a pawn race would become apparent in the event of 42...cxb4 43 c5 b3 (43...♔f8 44 c6 ♔e7 45 c7 and the pawn cannot be stopped by the king) 44 c6 b2 45 ♗c2! and Black can resign.

42 ...   ♔f8!

43 b5

The weakling on b3 becomes a monster on b5. 43 bxc5 is less good, when after 43...♔e7 44 c6 ♔d6 45 c7 ♔xc7 46 ♗e8 ♔d6 47 ♗xf7 ♘d3, threatening ...♘e5, Black saves himself. Since Black's king arrives first on the queenside, it is better for White to have a *protected* passed pawn there, especially one that is a file further from the kingside. The drawback to 43 b5 is that things get blocked, and this makes the win difficult.

43 ...   ♔e7

44 ♗c2!

It was possible for White to try for an immediate breakthrough with 44 b6. In his analysis in *Informator 62* Salov gives the more or less forced sequence 44...♔d6 45 ♗e8 ♘b3 46 ♗xf7 (46 ♔e2 ♘a5 47 ♗xf7 ♘xc4 leads to a transposition) 46...♘d2+ 47 ♔e2 ♘xc4 48 b7 ♔c7 49 ♗xe6 ♘d6.

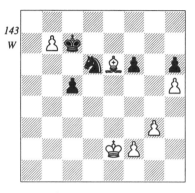

Now the attempt to create a passed pawn on the kingside is too slow: 50 g4 ♔xb7 (the most instructive, but 50...♘xb7 51 f4 ♔d6 52 ♗a2 ♔e7 53 g5 fxg5 54 hxg5 hxg5 55 h6 ♔f8 is simpler) 51 f4 ♔c7 52 g5 fxg5 53 fxg5 ♘e4! 54 gxh6 (54 g6 ♘g3+ and 55...♘xh5) 54...♘f6 55 ♗f5 ♔d6 56 h7 ♘xh7 57 ♗xh7 ♔e5 58 h6 ♔f6 (intending 59...♔g5) 59 ♗e4 ♔f7! reaches g8 with a bishop and "wrong" rook's pawn draw.

I don't know how deeply Salov examined 44 b6 during the game, but "common-sense" suggests that White should keep his pawn protected and secure on b5 until he has strengthened his game in other ways. For example, he can first centralise his king and advance his kingside pawns. The weakness of f7 won't go away, nor can Black do anything active to alter the assessment of the position.

44 ...   f5

The attempt to bring his knight back could lead to the following variation: 44...♘a2 45 g4 ♘b4 46 ♗e4 ♔d6 47 f4 e5 48 g5! fxg5 49 fxg5 hxg5 50 h6 and the h-pawn queens.

45	♔e1	♘a2
46	♔d2	♘b4
47	♗b1	♔d6

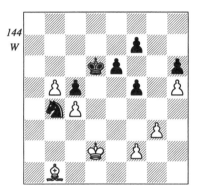

The alternative was 47...♔f6 when 48 ♔e3? ♔g5 wins the h-pawn, but White has good winning chances by heading with his king to the queenside, e.g. 48 ♔c3 ♔e5 49 ♔b3 (not 49 f4+ ♔d6 50 ♔b3 ♔c7 51 ♔a4 ♔b6 since White can't gain the opposition and oust the king from b6) 49...♔d4 50 b6 ♔e5 51 ♔a4 ♔d6 52 ♔b5 ♘c6 53 ♗d3 etc.

After the game move we have a highly interesting position. The knight on b4 is "stalemated" by the white pawns on c4 and b5 and

the bishop on b1. Similarly, the bishop is deprived of all moves by the black knight and pawn on f5. White cannot free his bishop with 48 ♗d3, as if minor pieces are exchanged then the position is too blocked to win. This is surprising in view of White's substantial structural advantage (protected passed pawn and doubled Black f-pawns.). However, analysis confirms it to be the case. Play could continue 48 ♗d3 ♘xd3 49 ♔xd3 f6! and White has no way to break through, e.g. 50 ♔e3 (if White's king tries to break through via a5, then Black advances his e-pawn at the right moment) 50...♔c7 51 ♔f4 ♔d6 52 f3 ♔c7 53 g4 fxg4 54 ♔xg4 (54 fxg4 ♔b6 holds) 54...♔b6 55 f4 ♔c7 56 f5 e5 57 ♔f3 ♔d7 58 ♔e4 ♔d6 59 ♔e3 ♔d7 60 ♔f3 ♔e7 61 ♔e4 ♔d6 with a draw.

Returning to the game position, White has to find another way to cut through the blockade. The logical plan is to put his king on f4 and, at the correct moment, play ♗xf5 as a sacrifice. Then White can create a second passed pawn on the kingside which will overstretch Black's defence.

Therefore, 48 ♔e3 is the obvious starting move. However, then 48...♔e5 follows, keeping the king out of f4. Chasing the king away with 49 f4+?? would be a fundamental error because it deprives White's own king of the f4-square. If White waits with 49 f3, hoping for 49...♔d6 50 ♔f4, then Black also has a waiting move, 49...f6!, and White has no way to progress. The reader may have noticed that since both minor pieces are inert, the position in some ways resembles a pure king and pawn endgame. The basic theme is that Black holds the opposition and stops White's king advancing. Salov was certainly aware of this and found a waiting move which gained him the opposition:

48 ♔e2!!

Black needs to be able to answer ♔e3 with ...♔e5, maintaining the opposition. Unfortunately, he has no good waiting move with his king (he cannot play ...♔e6 as there is a pawn on the square!). If 48...♔c7 or 48...♔e7, then 49 ♔e3 and 50 ♔f4 cannot be prevented. The upshot is that White gains the opposition and is able to carry out his winning plan.

48 ...   ♔e5
49 ♔e3

Now Black's king has to give way.

49 ...   ♔f6

Could Black have drawn with 49...f6, maintaining the opposition? No, since White also has the waiting move 50 f3! Now the attempt to keep it blocked with the pawn sacrifice 50...f4+ fails, e.g. 51 gxf4+ ♔d6 52 f5! (if he allows 52...f5 then the win is jeopardised) 52...e5 53 ♔d2 followed by putting the king on a4 and forcing the black king away from b6 with ♗e4 (zugzwang); then ♔a5 wins.

50 ♔f4   ♔e7

The king has to give way. If 50...e5+ 51 ♔e3 ♔g5 52 f4+ (Salov) wins, e.g. 52...exf4+ 53 gxf4+ ♔f6 (if 53...♔xh5, then 54 ♗xf5 and the bishop is dominant.) 54 b6 ♘c6 55 b7 ♔e6 56 ♗c2 and White manoeuvres his king over to b5. If Black's king follows he loses the f-pawn.

51 ♔e5!

Zugzwang forces a fresh weakness

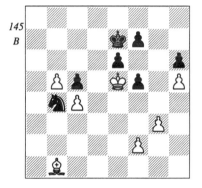

145
B

51 ...   f6+
52 ♔f4   ♔f7
53 b6

At last all is ready for the final phase.

53 ...   ♘c6
54 b7   ♔e7
55 ♗xf5!   ♔d6

Salov gives a long line to demonstrate the win after 55...exf5: 56 ♔xf5 ♔f7 57 g4 ♘b8 58 f3! (a matter of timing; he wants the knight to be on b8, not a6, when his king goes to the queenside, so he doesn't rush things with 58 f4)

58...♘a6 59 f4 ♘b8 60 g5 fxg5 61 fxg5 hxg5 62 ♔xg5 ♔g7 63 ♔f5 ♔h6 64 ♔e6 ♔xh5 65 ♔d6 ♔g6 66 ♔xc5 ♔f7 67 ♔d6 ♔e8 68 c5 ♔d8 69 c6 and wins.

The finish in the game was straightforward.

56 ♗e4 ♘b8 57 ♗g6 ♔c7 58 ♗f7 ♔d6 59 ♗e8 ♔e7 60 ♗b5 (dominating the knight) **60...♔d6 61 ♔e4 ♔c7 62 g4**

and Karpov resigned. The finish could be 62...♔xb7 63 f4 ♔c7 64 g5 fxg5 65 fxg5 hxg5 66 h6 and the pawn queens.

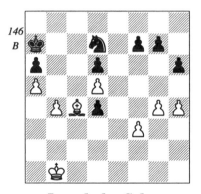

Ivanchuk – Salov
Buenos Aires 1994

Black's chances seem very poor: his king is tied to the defence of the a6-pawn and the d4-pawn is fatally weak. His only hope is to block the position, when the value of the bishop will be diminished and the white king kept at bay.

32 f4

Keeping the knight out of e5.

32 ...   ♘f6

33 g5   ♘h5!
34 gxh6   gxh6
35 f5

A significant victory for Black. The f-pawn has been forced to f5, where it blocks the action of the bishop and denies the white king a possible entry point on the kingside. The chances of a successful blockade increase.

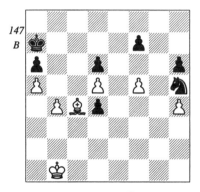

35 ...   ♘f6
36 ♔c2   ♘d7
37 ♔d3   ♘e5+
38 ♔xd4   f6
39 ♗e2   ♔b7

Black has achieved his best defensive set up and now waits.

40 ♔c3   ♔a7
41 b5

Salov criticises this move and recommends 41 ♔b3. However, after 41...♘d7! 42 ♔a4 ♔b7 43 b5 axb5+ 44 ♔xb5 ♘c5 Black has achieved a blockade on the queenside. Whether or not such a position can be won for White will be discussed at move 43.

41 ...   axb5

42 ♔b4

It now appears that Black is doomed, e.g. 42...♔b7 43 ♔xb5 ♔a7 44 a6 with zugzwang (if 44...♘d7 45 ♔c6 or 44...♔a8 45 ♔b6 ♔b8 46 a7+ ♔a8 47 ♗b5 with inevitable mate. Despite this, Salov finds a defence. From the above variation it can be established that White wins if he gets his king to b5 with the knight still on e5. So Black played

42 ...   ♔a6!!

Shutting the king out of b5.

43 ♗xb5+

If 43 ♗f1, waiting, then 43...♘c4 is simplest. After the text-move, the bishop obstructs its own king.

43 ...   ♔b7

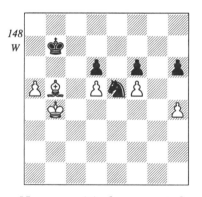

148
W

Now a critical moment has been reached. If White could put his bishop on e2 and play ♔b5 he would win, even if it were Black's move (see note to 42 ♔b4). However, Salov had planned the defence 44 ♗e2 ♘d7! 45 ♔b5 ♘c5. In *Informator 62* he claims this is a complete blockade. However,

White can get his bishop in "round the back" via h5. After 46 ♗h5 ♘a6 47 ♗f7 (47 ♗e8? ♘c7+) Black has two defensive tries:

a) 47...♘c5 48 ♗e8 ♘a6 49 ♗c6+ ♔a7 50 ♗a8! ♘c7+ (or 50...♘b8 51 h5! ♔xa8 52 ♔b6 wins) 51 ♔c6 ♘xa8 52 ♔xd6 and wins.

b) 47...♘c7+! 48 ♔c4! ♔a6 49 ♔d4 ♔xa5 50 ♔e4 ♔b5 51 ♔f4 ♔c5 52 ♔g4 ♘xd5 53 ♔h5 ♘e3 54 ♔g6 ♘g4 55 ♗b3 d5 56 ♗d1 ♘e3 57 ♗f3 d4 58 ♔xf6 and now Black loses after 58...♘xf5? 59 ♔xf5 ♔d6 60 ♔g6 ♔e7 61 ♔xh6 ♔f8 62 ♔h7! d3 63 h5 d2 64 h6 ♔f7 65 ♗d1 ♔f8 66 ♗b3 d1♕ 67 ♗xd1 ♔f7 68 ♗b3+ ♔f8 69 ♗c4 winning for White. However, he can draw with 58...♔d6 59 ♗e4 ♘g4+ 60 ♔g6 ♔e7, etc.

Although this analysis by no means exhausts the possibilities in the position, it is clear that White has some winning chances. In the game he missed his chance.

44 h5?

A very unnatural move, putting the pawn on a white square and closing h5 as an entry point for his king or bishop.

44 ...   ♘f3

45 ♗e2   ♘d4

This knight manoeuvre is directed against White's plan of putting his king on b5, when he would win as indicated at move 42.

46 ♗d3   ♔c7!

If 46...♔a7 then 47 ♔c4 ♘f3 48 ♗e2 ♘e5+ 49 ♔b5 achieves

White's winning set-up, but if now 47 ♔c4 then 47...♘f3 48 ♔b5 ♘d4+ 49 ♔a6 ♘b3! keeps the draw (Salov). White cannot progress, e.g. 50 ♗c4 ♘c5+ 51 ♔a7 ♘e4 52 a6? ♘g3 and White could lose because he has buried his king.

47 ♔c3 ♘f3 48 ♗f1 ♘e5 49 ♔b4 ♘f3 50 ♗e2 ♘d4 51 ♗d3 ♘f3 52 ♗e4 ♘d4 53 ♔c4 ♘e2 54 ♗f3 ♘g3 55 ♗g4 ♘e4 56 ♔b5

and White gave up his winning attempt. After 56...♘c3+ he has made no progress.

Judging from the last two games, Salov is happy to be either hammer or anvil in blocked endgames!

7 Defence in rook and pawn endgames

According to the old chess proverb, "all rook and pawn endgames are drawn". While this is a very dubious statement, if taken literally, it does point towards a vital piece of advice: if you are in trouble, seek salvation in a rook and pawn endgame! But why should it be a good idea to head for a rook endgame rather than, say, a minor piece endgame?

The answer rests in the enormous strength of the rook. It's ability to move swiftly from one side of the board to another and attack any square on rank or file makes it considerably more powerful than the bishop or knight. Therefore, an active rook can often give fully adequate counterplay for either a minus pawn or a serious defect in the pawn structure. A minor piece, on the other hand, even if it is well or even excellently placed, is much less likely to give sufficient compensation for a missing pawn.

It is normally recommended that a player a pawn down should aim to exchange pawns but not pieces, thus bringing him closer to the drawing haven of a pawnless endgame. However, at the same time it is also true that the more pieces there are on the board, the less scope there is for the rook to demonstrate its power. Only when the other pieces begin to vanish does the rook have the ability to become a juggernaut which can thunder from one side of the board to another. That is why, despite the apparent paradox, a player facing, for example, a position with a rook and bishop each can often increase the activity of his game by exchanging the bishops. Less sometimes means more!

Rook endgames are therefore fast moving and dynamic, which reduces the importance of static features such as a better pawn structure or an extra pawn. In contrast, positions with several pieces on the board or pure minor piece endgames tend to be slower and more measured, with the emphasis on material and pawn structure.

Of course, we are talking very generally here when every case has to be examined and judged according to its specific features. Sometimes a rook is miserable and constricted, and the complete opposite of the swift-footed warrior described above. But the emphasis in this chapter is on the dynamic nature of the rook.

Activity is the key

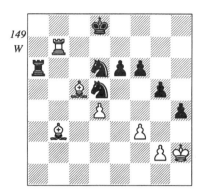

Gelfand – Kosashvili
Tyniste n.Orlici 1995

In our first example, White is a pawn down. As recommended above, he sought salvation in a rook and pawn endgame.

57 &xd5! exd5
58 &xd6 &xd6
59 &h3 &d7

If 59...f5, trying to keep the king out, then the reply 60 &g7 demonstrates why the rook is so powerful on the seventh rank.

60 &b5 &e7
61 f4!

Breaking up Black's pawns before they can be supported by the king. Every pawn exchange brings the draw closer.

61 ... gxf4

If 61...&e6 62 fxg5 fxg5 63 &g4.

62 &xh4 &e6
63 &g4!

It would be disastrous to allow 63...&f5 when, strategically speaking, the white king is cut off and

64...&e4, attacking d4, cannot be averted. Tactically speaking there would be no good way to prevent ...&h7 mate! After the text-move, Black succeeds in exchanging his f-pawn for the white g2-pawn, but the passed pawn he creates cannot advance.

63 ... &g7+
64 &xf4 &xg2
65 &b6+!

Chasing the king away from the defence of the d-pawn.

65 ... &f7
66 &b7+ &g6
67 &d7!

The ideal position for the rook. It ties down White's rook to the defence of the d-pawn and so makes it impossible for Black to drive away the white king from in front of the f-pawn. It also stops ...&f5. Therefore a draw becomes inevitable.

67 ... &g5
68 &f3

White has managed to set up an impenetrable blockade. He therefore waits.

68...&h5 69 &f4 &f5+ 70 &g4 &h5 71 &g3 &h6 72 &g4 &g5+ 73 &f4 &g6 74 &f3 &h5 75 &g3

and a draw was agreed.

Rooks belong behind passed pawns

It is a well respected principle that a rook belongs behind a passed pawn. This applies whether it be a "friendly" or "enemy" pawn. If it is a friendly pawn, then every step of its journey can be supported and guarded by the rook; if it is an enemy pawn then it is kept under the closest surveillance and the opponent is prevented from putting *his* rook behind the pawn.

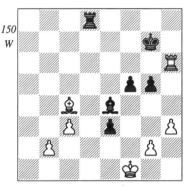

McDonald – Haikova-Maskova
Maidstone 1994

White is a pawn up, but everything else is bad for him. His queenside passed pawns are ineffective, while Black's passed pawn has already reached e3. The black bishop on e4 is dominant, and there is an immediate threat of ...♖d2 followed by ♗xg2+, creating passed pawns in the centre which would easily win the game. To add to White's misery, his rook is hanging.

However, the attack on the rook at least helps him to find the correct move. Where should it go? Maybe to b6 to defend the queenside pawns against 43...♖d2? No!

The priority, indeed the only path to safety, is to prevent Black acquiring connected passed pawns. This is achieved by...

43 ♖e6!

...which confirms our principle above.

43 ... ♖d2
44 g3!

If White had gone wrong with 43 ♖b6? on the previous move then Black could now have advanced the f-pawn, creating a second passed pawn. With the rook on e6, 44...f4?? drops the bishop; nor can Black's bishop move without losing the e3-pawn.

44 ... ♖xb2
45 ♖e7+ ♔f8

Forced, since 45...♔f6 46 ♖e6+ ♔g7 47 ♖e7+ etc. keeps the king shut out.

46 ♖e5!

Keeping the rook behind the passed pawn.

46 ... ♖c2
47 ♗b5!

So that 47...♖xc3 won't attack the bishop and can therefore be answered with 48 ♔e2, freeing the king from the first rank.

47 ... ♔g7

Now the bishop has been forced away from c4 the blockade on the e-file has been weakened and so the king tries to break out again.

48 ♖e6 ♔f7
49 ♖e5 ♔f6
50 ♖e8 ♖xc3?

Or 50...♗g2+ 51 ♔e1 ♗xh3 52 ♖xe3 is equal. However, as pointed

out by John Nunn, 50...♖g2 51 g4
(51 ♖xe4? ♖f2+) 51...♖b2 52 gxf5
(otherwise ...♗g2+ and then ...f4)
52...♔xf5, intending ...♔f4 followed
by ...♗f3, looks more dangerous.
If White responds to this plan by
bringing his bishop to g4 then 53
♗d7+ ♔f4 54 ♗g4 ♗d3+ 55 ♔g1
♖b1+ 56 ♔h2 ♗e4 57 ♖f8+ ♔e5 58
♖e8+ ♔d5 leaves him facing the
threat of 59...♖h1+ 60 ♔g3 ♖g1+
61 ♔h2 ♖g2+. Black evidently
has good winning chances.

51 ♔e2   ♗g2

Black has no way to progress.

52 ♗d3

But not 52 ♖xe3? ♗f1+! winning.

52 ...   ♗xh3
53 ♖xe3   ♖a3
54 ♔f2   ♗g4
55 ♗c4   ♖xe3

and a draw was agreed. After
55 ♔xe3 the extra pawn is mean-
ingless.

Defence by stalemate and perpetual check

In the following position Black appears to be completely lost. He is
two pawns down and the white
pieces are on dominating squares.
In addition, there is an immediate
threat of 68 ♕xf6. However, Kramnik managed to weave a defence
out of two drawing threats: stalemate and perpetual check.

67 ...   ♕c1!!

If now 68 ♕xd8, then Black
forces stalemate with 68...♕h1+

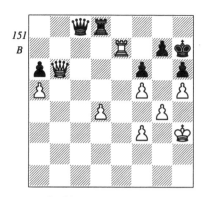

Gelfand – Kramnik
Sanghi Nagar 1994

69 ♔g3 ♕xf3+! 70 ♔h4 ♕xg4+!
(refusing to take no for an answer!). If 68 ♖xg7+ ♔xg7 69 ♕xd8,
destroying the stalemate, it is perpetual after 69...♕h1+ 70 ♔g3
♕g1+ 71 ♔f4 ♕c1+ 72 ♔e4 ♕c6+!
(denying the king escape via d5)
73 ♕d5 ♕c2+ etc. (Gelfand).

68 d5!

The best winning attempt. The
queen on b6 now covers the whole
diagonal a7-g1, which means that
Black cannot force perpetual check
(68...♕f1+ 69 ♔g3 and g1 is covered).

68 ...   ♕f4

Not 68...♖xd5? when 69 ♖xg7+
♔xg7 70 ♕b7+ ♔h8 71 ♕xd5 wins
as the white king can escape from
the checks.

69 ♔g2

Black draws after 69 ♕e3 ♕xe3
70 ♖xe3 ♖xd5 71 ♖a3 ♔g8: White
has an extra pawn, but if Black
keeps his rook on the 5th rank (he
plays ...♖b5 if the rook is attacked

by the white king) then White cannot break through.

Alternatively, if 69 ♕b3 then 69...♖b8! 70 ♕e3 ♕d6 71 ♕e6 ♕f4 72 ♕e4 ♕c1 and in view of the threat of ...♖b2, White had better force a draw with 73 d6 ♖b2 74 ♖xg7+ ♔xg7 75 ♕e7+ – this time he is the one to give perpetual check.

69 ... ♖c8!

Piece activity is the key. Here 69...♖xd5 would still have lost to 70 ♖xg7+ and 71 ♕b7+.

70 ♕xa6

Not 70 ♕xf6?? ♖b2+ and Black mates first, whilst 70 ♕f2 ♕c1 71 d6 ♕d1! picks up the d-pawn since 72 d7? loses to ...♖c2.

70 ... ♖c3!

The simplest way to draw. The alternative 70...♖c1 leads to some interesting play, e.g.

a) 71 d6 ♕d4! 72 ♕e2 (of course not 72 d7? ♖g1+ 73 ♔h3 ♕f2 mates) 72...♕g1+ 73 ♔h3 ♕h1+ 74 ♔g3 ♖g1+ 75 ♔f4 ♖g2! (intending ...♕h2+ or ...♕c1+) and White does best to force perpetual with 76 ♖xg7+ ♔xg7 77 ♕e7+.

b) 71 ♕e2 ♕d4 72 a6 ♖g1+ 73 ♔h3 ♕h1+ 74 ♔g3 ♖g1+ 75 ♔f4 ♖g2 and again Black's counterplay is so strong that White should force a draw with 76 ♖xg7+.

c) 71 ♖e2 ♕d4 72 ♖f2 ♕xd5!? intending 73...♖a1 to pick up the a-pawn, when White's extra kingside pawn is worthless.

71 ♕e2 ♕c1
72 ♕f2

Or 72...♖c2 wins the queen.

72 ... ♕d1!

Renewing the threat of ...♖c2 and attacking d5.

73 ♖e1 ♕xd5
74 ♖a1

Or 74 a6 ♖a3 and 75...♕a5 wins the a-pawn.

74 ... ♖d3!

Enticing the white rook to the second rank.

75 ♖a2 ♖xf3!
76 ♕xf3

and a draw was agreed in view of 76...♕xa2+ 77 ♕f2 ♕xa5. A brilliant defensive effort by Black!

Counterplay at all costs

Next we witness another Houdini-like escape by Kramnik, who is certainly one of the most resourceful defenders in the world.

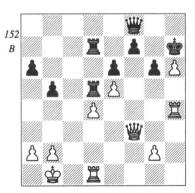

Bologan – Kramnik
Germany 1994

Black has already had to sacrifice one pawn to avert immediate mate along the h-file, but things still look grim for him. If he waits passively then White increases his advantage with g4, g5, ♖f4, ♖f1 and Black's position will soon become untenable. Realising that the middlegame is hopeless, Kramnik elects to sacrifice a second pawn and seek safety in the endgame.

31	...	f5!
32	exf6	♖f5
33	♕c6	♕d6!

Two pawns down, Black offers the exchange of queens. Although "all rook endgames are drawn", this one is actually losing. Nevertheless we can admire Kramnik's fighting spirit: he makes White's task as difficult as possible.

34 ♕xd6

Bologan also has no objection to an endgame.

| 34 | ... | ♖xd6 |
| 35 | ♖c1 | ♖d7 |

He cannot allow 36 ♖c7+.

36	♖c6	♖xf6
37	♖xa6	♖f1+
38	♔c2	♖f2+
39	♔b3	♖e2! *(D)*

Black's counterplay depends on this highly active rook. Note that he avoids 39...♖xg2 40 ♖xe6, since he hopes to win either the d-pawn or the g-pawn without giving up his e-pawn.

40 ♖h3!

Here the immediate 40 ♖b6? allows Black to activate his king after 40...g5! for example 41 ♖g4 ♖d5! intending ...♔xh6 or 41 ♖h3

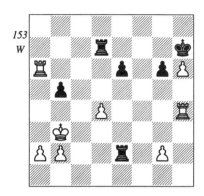

g4 42 ♖g3 (42 ♖h4 g3) 42...♖xd4 and again ...♔xh6 follows.

40 ... g5

If 40...♖xd4, then 41 ♖a7+ wins.

41 g4

This stops the g5-pawn advancing. Bologan plays very precisely and remains in control of the position.

41	...	♖e4
42	♖b6	♖exd4
43	♖xb5	♖xg4
44	a4	

Both sides have achieved their targets. Bologan has connected passed pawns which should win the game; Kramnik has swindling chances with his g-pawn.

44	...	♖g1
45	a5	g4
46	♖e3?	

The first sign of faltering by Bologan. He had an easy win with 46 ♖h4 e.g.

a) 46...♖d3+ 47 ♔a2 ♖h3 48 ♖b7+ ♔h8 (forced: if 48...♔g8 or 48...♔g6 then 49 ♖g7+ and 50 ♖xh3 wins a rook) 49 a6! ♖xh4 50 a7 and wins.

b) 46...g3 47 a6 and 48 ♖b7 will win.

The game continuation should win, but now it is more complex.

46 ...   ♖h1!
47 a6

If 47 ♖xe6, then 47...♖xh6 48 ♖xh6+ ♔xh6 and the black g-pawn advances, supported if necessary by ...♖g7.

47 ...   ♖h3!
48 ♖xh3   gxh3
49 ♖h5   ♖a7
50 ♖xh3   ♖xa6
51 ♔c4   ♖c6+
52 ♔b5 (D)

In *Informator 60*, Bologan gives the variation 52 ♔d4 ♖b6 53 b3 ♖b8 54 ♔e5 ♖b6 55 ♔f6 ♖c6 56 b4 ♖b6 57 ♖h4 ♖c6 58 b5 ♖b6 59 ♖h5 as "winning". Unfortunately he overlooks the defence 59...e5+! and Black draws, which serves as a reminder of the difficulty of rook and pawn endgames. Instead, at the end of this variation, White can indeed win with 59 ♖b4! (rather than 59 ♖h5?). As usual, the rook belongs behind the passed pawn. Black is in zugzwang and soon loses for example 59...♔g8 (59...♔xh6 60 ♖h4 mate) 60 ♔e5 ♔h7 61 ♔d4 ♔xh4 (the time wasted with 59...♔g8 is fatal) 62 ♔c5 ♖b8 63 ♔d6! (simplest) 63...♔g5 64 ♔xe6 and with the disappearance of the e-pawn all hope is gone.

52 ...   ♖c8
53 b4   e5
54 ♔b6?

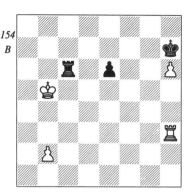

154
B

Incredibly, this throws away the win! Bologan points out the correct move 54 ♖e3! when White wins at the end of a complex variation: 54...♖e8 (giving up the e-pawn is equivalent to resignation) 55 ♔c5 ♔g6 (if 55...♔xh6 56 ♔d5 ♖b8 57 ♖e4 ♖b5+ 58 ♔c6 {or 58 ♔c4} 58...♖b8 59 b5 wins) 56 ♔d5 ♔f5 57 h7 ♖d8+ 58 ♔c6 ♖h8 (Bologan gives 58...♔f4, which leads by transposition to the same ending after 59 ♖e1 e4 60 ♖h1 ♖h8 61 b5 e3 62 b6 e2 63 b7 ♔f3 etc.) 59 ♖h3 ♔g4 60 ♖h1 e4 61 b5 e3 62 b6 e2 63 b7 ♔f3 64 ♖b1! ♔f2 65 b8♕ ♖xb8 66 ♖xb8 e1♕ 67 h8♕ and wins.

A difficult piece of analysis. It's no wonder that White failed to calculate it properly in the game.

Now Kramnik escapes with a draw.

54 ...   e4
55 b5   ♖e8
56 ♔a7?!   e3
57 ♖h1   e2
58 ♖e1   ♔xh6
59 b6   ♔g5

60 b7   ♔g4!

Not 60...♔f4? 61 ♖xe2! ♖xe2 62 b8♕ check! Now if White queens Black gives up his rook then plays ♔f3 with an immediate draw.

61 ♖xe2

and a draw was agreed. After 61...♖xe2 62 b8♕ ♖a2+ 63 ♔b7 ♖b2+ Black captures the queen. One question remains. What if White had played 56 ♔c7 rather than 56 ♔a7?

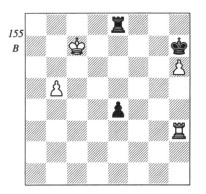

155
B

Then if play continues exactly as in the game White wins: 56...e3 57 ♖h1 e2 58 ♖e1 ♔xh6 59 b6 ♔g5 60 b7 ♔g4 61 ♖xe2! ♖xe2 62 b8♕ and because the king is on c7 rather than a7 there is no trick to pick up the queen.

However, Black can draw by activating his rook with 56...e3 57 ♖h1 e2 58 ♖e1 ♖e3! White cannot win e.g. 59 b6 ♖c3+ 60 ♔b8 ♖c2 61 b7 ♔xh6 62 ♖a1 (62 ♖b1 ♖b2 or 62 ♔a7 ♖a2+ 63 ♔b6 ♖b2+, checking the king away from the pawn or back to b8) 62...♔g5 63 ♔a7 ♖b2 64 ♖e1 (64 b8♕ ♖xb8 65

♔xb8 ♔f4) 64...♖a2+ 65 ♔b6 ♖b2+ 66 ♔c7 ♖c2+ 67 ♔d6 ♖b2 etc. with a draw.

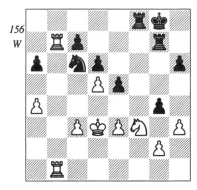

156
W

Kasparov – Anand
New York 1995

Kasparov thought he saw a straightforward win when he played...

31 dxc6

He had analysed 31...gxf3 32 gxf3 ♖xf3 33 ♖a7 ♖gg3 (or 33...d5 34 ♖bb7 ♖gg3 35 ♖b8+ ♔h7 36 ♖xc7+ ♔g6 37 ♖g8+ ♔h5 38 ♖xg3 ♖xg3 39 ♖e7 wins) 34 ♖xc7 ♖xe3+ 35 ♔c4 ♖xc3+ 36 ♔d5 and wins. White's king can be driven all the way to d8 by the black rooks but then it will be safe from checks and the c-pawn will quickly decide the game.

However, Anand had a little surprise for the World Champion.

31 ...   e4+!

This pawn sacrifice opens the centre and ensures that the white king won't have a safe refuge on d8.

32	♔xe4	gxf3
33	gxf3	♖e7+
34	♔d4	♖xf3
35	e4	

If 35 ♖a7? then 35...♖fxe3 intending to give perpetual check by 36...♖7e4+ and 37...♖e5+.

35	...	♖xh3
36	♖xc7?	

In time pressure, White lets Black escape with a draw. The correct 36 ♖a7!, going after the a-pawn, should win. Then 36...♖h4 37 ♖e1! defends against the black rooks and prepares ♖xa6 followed by the advance of the a-pawn. Note that the impatient 37 ♖bb7? allows 37...♖hxe4+ 38 ♔d3 ♖4e5! 39 ♖xc7 ♖xc7 40 ♖xc7 ♖c5! and Black holds the draw.

36	...	♖xc7
37	♖b8+	♔f7
38	♖b7	

How can Black save himself?

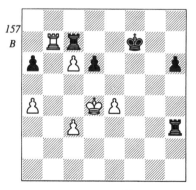

38	...	♖e7!

The only move. Kasparov now wins a pawn but it proves worthless.

39 c7 ♖xc7 40 ♖xc7+ ♔e6 41 ♖a7 h5 42 ♖xa6 ♖h1 43 ♖a8 h4 and a draw was agreed. In the *British Chess Magazine* Rogers gives the possible finish 44 a5 h3 45 ♔c4 h2 46 ♖h8 (White is a tempo short to win) 46...♖a1 47 ♖xh2 ♖xa5 etc. and the extra pawn cannot be exploited.

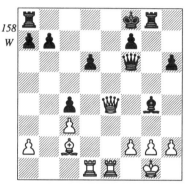

Yusupov – Korchnoi
Madrid 1995

Black threatens ...♗xd1 and the obvious 23 ♖d4? loses to 23...♗f3, so White forced an endgame with

23	♕d4!	♕xd4
24	♖xd4	♗f3
25	g3	

Yusupov has escaped from the danger and suddenly finds himself in a rather pleasant position. He will regain his pawn by force and his rooks are much more active than his opponent's. Can he strike a telling blow before Black succeeds in mobilising his pieces?

Black now has an important choice. He has to return his extra pawn, since 25...d5 26 ♖e3 ♗g4 27 ♖xd5 regains the pawn anyway with evident loss of time by Black, so the question is, should Black save the c4-pawn or the d6-pawn? At first, it seems to make more sense to defend the c4-pawn with 25...b5 or 25...♖c8 rather than save the weakling on d6, which is the feeblest of all pawns: a backward pawn on an open file.

However, in this instance such reasoning is fallacious because it sees no further than the static features of the position: it's nicer to have an intact queenside pawn structure than a broken one. The reality is that dynamically speaking, the d6-pawn is more valuable than the c4-pawn. If Black plays 25...♖c8 then 26 ♖xd6 and the white rook has penetrated into Black's position with the threats of 27 ♖xh6 and 27 ♖d7, seizing the seventh rank. The d6-pawn may be more vulnerable and more isolated than the c4-pawn, but it carries out an important function in restraining the activity of the white rooks. The c4-pawn is a pawn and valuable as such; the d6-pawn is both a pawn and a obstacle to the white rooks.

> **25 ...   ♖d8!**

Korchnoi knows these things!

> **26 ♖xc4   ♔g7!**

Now Black is ready to activate his king's rook with 27...♖ge8.

> **27 ♖f4   ♗d5!**

It's vital to restrain the activity of White's pieces. If Black plays

the careless 27...♗c6 then White will have time for 28 ♗b3 and 29 ♖e7, putting Black under intolerable pressure. Now, however, the a2-pawn is attacked, and all danger would be past for Black after 28 a3 ♖ge8 or 28 c4 ♗e6. So White has to acquiesce in the exchange of bishops, when, as we know, all rook endings are drawn...

> **28 ♗b3   ♗xb3**
> **29 axb3   ♖ge8**

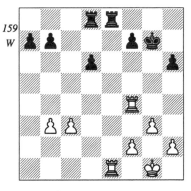

> **30 ♖xe8**

The problem of exchanging. After the exchange of one pair of rooks it is easier for the white king to advance towards the action as he no longer has to fear a sudden attack by the combined action of the enemy rooks. On the other hand, the black king's approach is also made easier. White could have played **30 ♖a1 a6 31 ♖b4** when after **31...♖d7** he would need to find a plan that proves the rook on b4 to be more valuable than the rook on e8. Such a plan would need the assistance of the white king who, although cut off from the queenside along the e-file, could stretch Black's defences by advancing up the kingside to f5 or even h5, attacking the h6-pawn.

A possible continuation is to play **32 ⌐b6** followed by bringing the other rook up to attack the b-pawn.

Black could then reply 32...⌐f8, centralising his king and hoping eventually to bring it to c7, where it defends both the b7 and d6 pawns. Play could continue **33 ⌐a4 ⌐8e7** (interesting is 33...⌐c7, provoking 34 c4. Although this secures white's pawn, it circumscribes the action of his rook on the fourth rank and makes the black kingside safe from sudden attack with ⌐h4 or ⌐f4. After 34...⌐d7 35 ⌐ab4 ⌐ee7, Black can play his king to c7 with a safe game. In contrast, the attempt to counterattack with 33...⌐e1+? fails after 34 ⌐g2 ⌐c1 35 c4 ⌐c2 36 ⌐ab4 ⌐e7 37 ⌐xd6 ⌐ee2 38 ⌐f6.) **34 ⌐d4 ⌐e6 35 ⌐d5 ⌐e7 36 c4 ⌐d8 37 ⌐g2 ⌐c7**, and black should draw comfortably.

The reader will by now have realised how apparently simple endgames contain a great deal of poison. It would only require a slight slip for Black to find himself in a fatal bind.

30 ...   ⌐xe8
31 ⌐f1

After 31 ⌐a4, Black should avoid the passivity of 31...a6 32 ⌐b4 ⌐e7 33 ⌐b6 ⌐d7 34 ⌐g2. Activity is the key to all endgames and instead he should counterattack with 31...⌐e1+ 32 ⌐g2 ⌐b1! 33 ⌐b4 (33 b4 a6 with 34...⌐b3 to follow) 33...b6 and the black rook outstrips its adversary.

31 ...   ⌐e5

The correct plan. Black has no intention of letting his rook be tied down.

32 ⌐d4   ⌐c5!

Again it was possible to sink into passivity with 32...d5? when 33 ⌐d3! ⌐f6 34 f4 ⌐f5 (White's 33rd move ruled out 34...⌐e3) 35 ⌐e2 followed by bringing the king to d4 gives White good winning chances.

33 c4   ⌐c6
34 ⌐e2   ⌐b6

For the moment this is the best square for the rook, defending d6 and attacking b3.

35 ⌐d3   ⌐f6
36 ⌐d2   ⌐e6
37 ⌐c3

The white king frees the rook from its defensive duty. Now there is the threat of 38 ⌐d5 and 39 ⌐h5, winning the h6-pawn, so Black must again seek active play. This counterplay will rest on the fact that the white king's journey to c3 has left his kingside undefended.

37 ...   ⌐a6!
38 ⌐e3+

If 38 ⌐d5 ⌐a2. Now before making another winning attempt Yusupov repeats the position to clarify his thoughts and gain time on the clock.

38	...	♚f6
39	♖f3+	♚e6
40	♖e3+	♚f6
41	♖f3+	♚e6
42	g4	♖a2

Directed against the intended 43 ♖h3. White will have to try this move as it is his only winning attempt, but first he improves the position of his king.

| 43 | ♚d4 | ♖b2 |

An ideal post for the rook, attacking b3 and f2.

| 44 | ♚e4 | a5 |

Permanently fixing the weakness on b3 and preparing later on to break up White's pawns with ...a4.

| 45 | ♖h3 | ♖e2+! |

Much better than the immediate 45...♖xf2 46 ♖xh6+. Korchnoi forces White's king to an inferior square before capturing the pawn.

46	♚f3	♖b2
47	♚e4	♖e2+
48	♚d3	♖xf2
49	♖xh6+	♚d7!

Black demonstrates impeccable technique. 49...♚e5 would be bad after 50 ♖h5+, so the king moves over to the queenside, where the final battle will be fought.

| 50 | ♖h5 | ♖f3+ |
| 51 | ♚c2 | a4! |

This liquidation deprives Yusupov of any winning chances.

52	bxa4	♖f4
53	♚d3	♖xg4
54	♖f5	♖h4!

White would have some slight chances after 54...♖g7 55 h4. Instead Korchnoi is true to the spirit of his play throughout the game and temporarily sacrifices a pawn to keep his rook active and activate his king.

| 55 | ♖xf7+ | ♚c6 |
| 56 | ♖f2 | ♚c5! |

Planning to win the c-pawn with ...♖h3+. So Yusupov forces a draw.

57	♖f5+	♚c6
58	♖f2	♚c5
59	♖f5+	♚c6

and a draw was agreed.

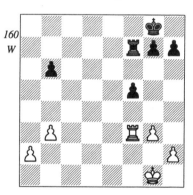

K. Arkell – Harley
London 1996

White began with
31 a4
Fixing the black pawn on b6. The immediate 31 ♖c3 also deserved attention when 31...b5?? 32 ♖f8+ ♖f8 33 ♖xf8+ ♚xf8 34 a4 gives White a winning pawn endgame. 31...g5 would also be bad for Black after 32 ♖c8+ ♚g7 33

♖b8 ♖f6 when the white rook dominates its adversary. If Black tries 31...♖d7 then 32 a4 ♔f7 33 ♔f2 gives White serious winning chances. He plans 34 ♔e3, 35 ♖c6 (forcing ...♖b7) and then ♔d4, when the king is poised to attack the b6-pawn after ♔c4 etc. Black is dogged by the fact that he can never exchange rooks, for example, 33...g5 34 ♔e3 ♔e6? 35 ♖c6+ ♖d6 36 ♖xd6+ ♔xd6 is winning for White, nor can he afford ever to give up his sickly b-pawn and seek counterplay on the kingside. One example of this is 33...♖d2+ 34 ♔e3 ♖xh2 35 ♖c6 when Black must choose between allowing White connected passed pawns on the queenside after 36 ♖xb6, playing 35...♖h6 when 36 ♖xh6 gxh6 is another winning pawn endgame for White, or continuing 35...b5, when White can choose between 36 axb5, which probably wins, or 36 a5, planning to pick up the b5-pawn later and maintain connected passed pawns.

Black's best defence looks a little odd, but he should answer 31 ♖c3 with 31...♖b7! followed by the centralisation of the king to d6. Then neither 32 ♔f2 ♔f7 33 ♔e3 ♔e6 34 ♔d4 ♔d6 nor 32 ♖c6 ♔f7 33 a4 ♔e7 34 b4 ♖a7 35 ♖xb6 ♖xa4 should trouble him.

[*Typesetter's note:* 32 ♖c4 ♔f7 33 ♖b4 ♔e6 34 a4 is an interesting try, for example 34...♔d6 35 a5 b5 36 a6 ♖a7 37 ♖xb5 winning a pawn. However, the odd-looking

34...g6 may draw, so that the f5-pawn doesn't hang. The pawn ending after 35 ♖b5 ♔d6 36 a5 ♔c6 looks drawn by one tempo.]

31 ...   g6?!

It was also possible to bring the king to the queenside without more ado: 31...♔f8 32 ♖c3 (32 ♔f2 and 32 b4 are answered by the immediate centralisation ...♔e7 and ...♔d6) 32...♖b7! followed by ...♔e7 and ...♔d6.

32 ♖c3!

A serious error is 32 b4? since after 32...♖a7 33 ♖a3 the white rook has been forced into a passive role defending his a-pawn. This means that the black b-pawn is no longer in danger, and Black's king can be centralised without harassment. A possible continuation is 33...♔f7 34 a5 bxa5 35 bxa5 (35 ♖xa5 ♖b7) 35...♖a6! (stopping the passed pawn getting any further) 36 ♔f2 ♔e6 37 ♔e3 ♔e5 38 ♔d3 g5 (38...♔d5 also draws) and if White tries to force the passed pawn through he could even run into trouble: 39 ♔c4 f4 40 ♔b5 ♖a8 41 a6 ♔e4 (41...fxg3 42 ♖xg3!) 42 gxf4 gxf4 43 a7 f3 44 ♔b6 f2 45 ♖a1 and Black can draw by forcing White to give up his rook for the f-pawn, or he can play to win with 45...h5!? Of course, White does best to avoid the line with 39 ♔c4 altogether and acquiesce in a draw.

The fact that White's rook is poorly placed on a3 is another exception to the rule that "rooks belong behind passed pawns".

32 ...　　　　　　🨢a7?

Here, however, the above rule still applies. Black should play 32...🨢b7! followed by centralising his king. Then the position after 33 b4? 🨢a7! 34 🨢a3 has already been discussed in the note to White's 32nd move (we have transposed to it here after having the moves ...🨢b7 and 🨢c3 thrown in). Black draws comfortably. If instead White centralises his king, then Black copies him, while if 33 🨢c6, then Black defends as in the final note to White's 31st move. In no case should Black lose.

33 🨢c6!

White could also play 33 🨔f2! The point is that 33...🨔f7 34 🨔e3 🨔e6, which would be satisfactory for Black with the rook on b7, now simply loses a pawn to 35 🨢c6+. Black would have to play 34...🨔e7 instead, but then 35 🨢c6 🨢b7 36 🨔d4 🨔d7 37 🨔d5 puts White's king in a dominant position, with the threat of 38 🨢d6+ and 39 🨔c6. However, the move played should also win.

33 ...　　　　　　b5

Black sees that after 33...🨢b7 34 🨔f2 etc. he will end up in the variation examined in the previous note, so he makes a bid for freedom.

34 axb5　　　　　🨔f7
35 b6??

All rook endgames are drawn! White would win easily after 35 b4! Then after 35...🨢a1+ 36 🨔f2 🨢b1 37 🨢c4! the b5-pawn runs

home, or 35...🨢a4 36 🨢c4 🨔e6 37 b6 🨢a6 38 b7 🨢b6 39 🨢c6+! wins. Finally 35...🨢a4 36 🨢c4 🨔e7 37 b6 🨢a6 38 🨢c6 🨔d7 39 b7! decides. If Black defended passively then White could always bring up his king and force the win. The careless game move allows the black rook to get behind the b6-pawn, and it suddenly becomes a drawn position.

35 ...　　　　　　🨢a5!
36 🨢c7+　　　　　🨔e6
37 🨢xh7　　　　　🨢b5
38 b7　　　　　　🨢xb3
39 🨔f2　　　　　🨔e5

Here 39...g5 seems to be the easiest way to draw, e.g. 40 h4 gxh4 41 gxh4 🨔f6 42 h5 f4 43 🨔e2 f3+ (there are even other ways to draw) 44 🨔f2 🨔g5 etc. with a total draw.

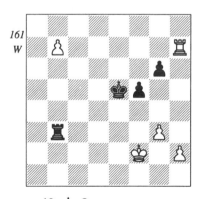

40 🨔e2

And now 40 h4! was the only chance for an advantage. However, we can set up two schematic positions that demonstrate how Black holds the draw:

Scenario 1

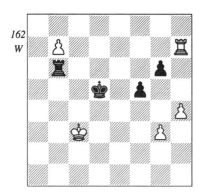

A draw. The white king can never break through the c4-barrier. Black plays his rook from b6 to b1 and back again. If 1 ♖d7+ ♔e6 2 ♖g7 ♔d5 etc. White can try 1 ♖g7 ♖b1 2 ♖xg6 ♖xb7, but the endgame is drawn.

If the white king is on e3 rather than c3, then Black puts his king on e5 and shuts him out of f4.

Scenario 2

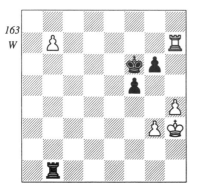

In this position the white king has sought shelter on h3. Black's king has moved to f6 to anticipate any attempted breakthrough with h5. Black has no problems here, and with the move plays 1...♖b3! threatening 2...f4 and so forcing a repetition after 2 ♔g2 ♖b2+ 3 ♔h3 ♖b3 etc., or an eventual transference to scenario one after 2 ♔g2 ♖b2+ 3 ♔f3 etc.

| 40 ... | g5 |

Black decides to clarify the position.

| 41 ♔d2 | f4! |
| 42 g4 | |

If 42 gxf4+ then 42...gxf4! draws in the same style as described in the note at move 39. Now Black's strong passed pawn and very active king and rook ensure the draw.

42 ...	f3!
43 ♖f7	♔e4
44 ♖c7	f2
45 ♖e7+	♔f4

Avoiding the "trap" 45...♔f3 46 ♖e3+ ♖xe3 47 b8♕ ♖e2+ (or 47...f1♕ 48 ♕g3+ ♔e4 49 ♕xe3+ and 50 ♕xg5+ wins) 48 ♔d3 f1♕ 49 ♕g3 mate! Of course, I do not need to point out that this variation isn't forced, and moves such as 47...f1♘+ and 48 ...♖e3+ are possible. Black prefers to avoid any risk.

| 46 ♔e2 | ♖b2+ |

and a draw was agreed.

Schematic thinking

In the analysis at move 40 in the previous game, there was an example of schematic thinking. It was possible to give two positions which could arise at some future point after 40 h4 without giving the exact intervening moves. Here is a more detailed explanation of this important thinking technique.

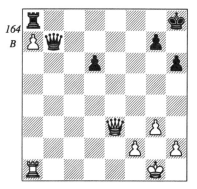

Rowson – McDonald
London 1995

First of all we will carry out a very simple check to see if the black pieces can undertake anything active.

a) The black rook has to stay on the first rank, and even moving from a8 could be dangerous e.g. 45...♔g8 46 h4 ♔h8 47 ♔h2 ♖f8 48 ♖d1! ♖a8 49 ♖xd6 and White wins after both 49...♕xa7 50 ♖d8+! ♔h7 51 ♕d3+ g6 52 ♖d7+ and 49...♖xa7 50 ♖d8+ ♔h7 51 ♕d3+ g6 52 h5! ♕g7 53 hxg6+ ♕xg6 54 ♖h8+! ♔g7 55 ♖g8+. This variation shows that Black should keep his rook passively on a8 to prevent White suddenly activating his own rook. Only if

White weakens himself in a serious way can the rook hope to emerge effectively.

However, we don't really need variations to convince ourselves that the black rook has only a passive role. What about the queen?

b) The black queen is tied to the b7 and c7 squares. This is because White wins if he can get his queen to the b6 square. For example, if Black plays 45...♕f7? then 46 ♕b6! (threatens 47 ♕b8+) 46...♔h7 47 ♕b8 ♕g8 48 ♕xd6 or 48 ♕xg8+ with an easily won rook and pawn endgame. The black queen could also prevent ♕b6 on the c6-square, but then it has lost contact with the a7-pawn: this could allow the white rook to be freed for aggressive duty, much as we saw in variation a.

Therefore the black queen has a purely defensive role, and can only leave the sphere of the white passed pawn if a chance for perpetual check presents itself. This can only happen if White is extremely careless. Finally, what about the black passed pawn?

c) The d6-pawn is so feeble that it hardly deserves the impressive title of passed pawn. Black would gladly swap it for an extra kingside pawn, say on f7, which would make his king much safer. In fact, if the d6-pawn were on f7 I cannot see any clear winning chances for White. Black should avoid playing ...d5, for two good reasons. As we have seen above, Black's queen has to stay on b7, so d5 would block its diagonal influence and therefore makes White's king much safer from perpetual check. Also, on d5 the pawn could suddenly be captured by the lateral move ♖a5. For example, 45...d5 46 ♕d4 ♔g8 47 h4 ♔h8 48 h5 ♔g8 49 ♖a5 ♔h8 50 ♖xd5 ♕xa7 51 ♖d8+ ♔h7 52 ♕d3+ and mates.

Such a lateral attacking plan fails with the pawn on d6: ♖a6?? is answered by ...♕xa6!

So, we can conclude that there is no possible active plan for Black. He can neither advance his passed pawn nor free his pieces from the bind of the a7-pawn.

So White doesn't have to think in terms of variations. In his mind he can visualise a winning position without worrying about the intermediate moves. Here is the ideal set up for White's pieces:

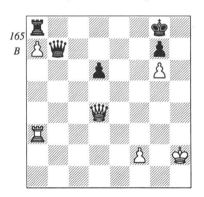

It is obvious that Black will be quickly mated in this position after ♕h4 or ♖h3. Play could end

1...d5 (what else?) 2 ♕h4 ♕c7+ (2...♖xa7 3 ♕d8 mate) 3 ♔g2 ♕d6 4 ♕h7+ ♔f8 5 ♖e3 and mate on h8.

How can White bridge the gap between the game position and the ideal position? Once you know where you are heading it is very easy.

First White plays ♕d4! putting his queen on its ideal square: from here it interacts with the important defensive squares a7 and f2, and the attacking squares b6, d6 and g7. Then White plays h4 and ♔h2. This is the safest square for the white king – it is protected laterally by the f2 pawn and is out of range of the black queen. Then White should play ♖a3, stopping Black ever playing ...♕f3 and preparing to swing the rook over to the kingside, especially the h-file, when appropriate. Then the pawn attack should start. White plays g4 and g5 breaking up Black's kingside pawn cover. Finally, we reach the diagram position, where White has forced open the h-file and put a pawn on g6. Black will quickly be mated.

Let's see how this works in practice: 45...♔g8 46 ♕d4 ♔h8 47 h4 ♔g8 48 ♔h2 ♔h8 49 ♖a3 ♔g8 50 g4 ♔h8 51 g5 hxg5 (if 51...h5, then 52 g6 and 53 ♖a5 wins) 52 hxg5 ♔g8 53 g6 and we have reached the ideal position.

45 ...   ♔g8

46 ♕e6+

This check doesn't achieve anything but neither does it do any harm; who knows, perhaps Black will play 46...♛f7? when 47 ♛xd6 ♖xa7(?) 48 ♛b8+ wins.

46	...	♚h8
47	♛e3	♚g8
48	h4	♚h8
49	♛d4	♚g8
50	h5	

An obvious move, increasing White's space advantage on the kingside. However, it was time to stop playing "good positional moves" and work out a winning plan, like that described at move 45 above.

After 50 h5 the plan of putting a pawn on g6 is much harder to achieve. If White ever plays g5, Black simply captures it, because it is no longer supported by the h-pawn. This means that in order to carry out a pawn attack White has to play f4 to support the g-pawn, but in that case the white king is left considerably more exposed, and Black gains counter-chances.

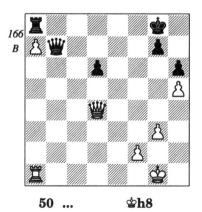

166
B

50 ...   ♚h8

Is it still possible for White to win? Before 50 h5 we could set up the ideal position for White without worrying about tactical nuances. Now things are much more complicated.

Let's begin by putting White's pieces on their optimum squares: 51 ♖a3 ♚g8 52 ♚h2 ♚h8. And here g4 is necessary sooner or later, so let's play it immediately: 53 g4 ♚g8.

Now White has an important choice. Should he play 54 f4, bolstering the attack, but exposing his king?

First of all, suppose that White avoids 54 f4. Then play continues 54 ♖a5 ♚h7! (if 54...♚h8 55 g5 hxg5 56 h6 gives a winning attack, while the attempt to counterattack with 54...♛f3 rebounds after 55 ♖f5! ♛b7 56 ♛c4+ ♚h8 57 ♖f7, when White has activated his rook with decisive effect). Apparently White has no way to strengthen his position here.

It follows that White has to use his f-pawn aggressively. After 54 f4 Black has a choice of plans:

a) Black defends passively.

a1) 54...♚h8 55 g5 hxg5 56 h6 (with the threat 57 hxg7+ ♛xg7 58 ♖h3+ ♚g8 59 ♛d5+, winning a rook) 56...g4 (ruling out ♖h3. If instead 56...♚g8, then 57 hxg7 gxf4 58 ♖h3 wins) 57 ♖a5! (with the same idea as last move) 57...d5 58 ♖xd5 ♖xa7 59 hxg7+ ♛xg7 60 ♖h5+ ♚g8 61 ♛d8+ ♚f7 (61...♛f8 62 ♖h8+) 62 ♖f5+ ♚e6

63 ♕d5+ ♔e7 64 ♖e5+ ♔f8 65 ♕d8+ ♔f7 66 ♕e8+ ♔f6 67 ♕e6 mate.

a2) 54...♔h7 55 g5 hxg5 56 fxg5 ♔g8 (Black avoids the h8-square on pain of h6) 57 g6 (in fact 57 h6 also wins) and Black has no moves, for example 57...♔h8 58 h6 or 57...♕c6 58 ♖e3 ♕c2+ 59 ♔g3 ♖f8 60 ♕d5+ ♔h8 61 ♕f7! (not allowing 61...♕f2+) 61...♕c8 (61...♖xf7 62 ♖e8+ mates) 62 ♖a3! (or 62 ♕xf8+ ♕xf8 63 ♖b3 and 64 ♖b8 winning) 62...♖xf7 63 gxf7 ♕a8 64 f8♕+ and wins.

b) 54...♖c8! (Black should defend actively; now he threatens 55...♖c2+). After 55 ♕d2 (planning either 56 ♕a2+ or 56 a8♕) 55...♔h8 56 ♕a2 ♖a8 White's queen has been sidelined and his progress is stymied.

The purpose of this example has been to demonstrate schematic thinking and the use of pawns to increase an advantage in an 'evolutionary' way. However, as John Nunn points out, things are much simpler. White can exploit a tactical nuance to win directly after 51 ♔h2 ♔g8 (51...♔h7 52 ♖a6) 52 ♖a6! ♔h7 (52...♔h8 53 ♖xd6 wins at once; 52...d5 is bad as explained above) 53 ♕d3+ ♔h8 54 ♕xd6 ♖xa7 55 ♖b6 picking up the queen.

51 ♖e1   ♕f7

Here the a pawn is immune: 51...♕xa7? 52 ♖e8+! wins the queen or mates after 52...♔h7 53 ♕d3+. Also mating is 51...♖xa7

52 ♖e8+ and 53 ♕d3+. It was in order to set this trap that White squandered his chance of an easy win with 50 h5.

52 ♖a1

After 52 ♕xd6 ♕xa7 53 ♖e7 ♕a1+ Black defends, but he must avoid 52...♖xa7 53 ♕d8+! ♔h7 54 ♖e8 ♖a1+ 55 ♔g2 ♕b7+ (note if White had carelessly played 53 ♕b8+? Black could now win with 55...♕d5+ 56 f3 ♖a2+ 57 ♔h3 ♕xh5 mate) 56 f3 ♕b2+ 57 ♔h3 ♖h1+ 58 ♔g4 ♕b4+ 59 f4, and mate follows on h8.

52 ...   ♕b7

Black mustn't allow 53 ♕b6.

53	♕a4	♕f7
54	♕b5	♕c7!
55	♕a4	♕f7
56	♕a6	♕c7
57	♔g2	

White realises that Black won't let him get his queen to b6.

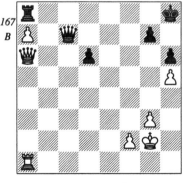

57	...	♔g8
58	♖a3	♔h8
59	♖a4	♔g8
60	♖a2	♔h8

61 Ra3   &g8
62 g4

At last White begins a pawn advance...

62 ...   &h8
63 Re3?

...but promptly blunders his a7-pawn.

63 ...   Wd7!

Capturing on a7 (either way) loses immediately to 64 Re8+, but now the g4-pawn is attacked, e8 is covered and ...Rxa7 is really threatened. White cannot allow 64...Wxg4+, so he has to acquiesce to a drawn queen and pawn endgame.

64 We2 Wxa7 65 Re8+ Rxe8 66 Wxe8+ &h7 67 Wg6+ &h8 68 Wxd6 Wb7+ 69 &g3 Wb3+ 70 f3 We3! (Black's queen slips behind the pawn cover to achieve perpetual check. Note how well placed Black's king is on h8. It defends the g7-pawn and is on the most sheltered square on the board, ruling out any cross checks by White's queen) **71 Wd8+ &h7 72 Wf5+ &h8 73 Wc8+ &h7 74 Wc2+ &h8 75 Wf2 We5+ 76 f4 Wc3+ 77 Wf3 We1+ 78 Wf2 Wc3+ 79 Wf3 We1+ 80 &h3 Wg1** and White eventually gave up his winning attempt.

Missed chances

In our final examples, the loser could have saved himself if he had believed in the drawing magic of rook and pawn endgames.

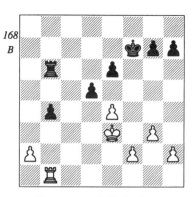

Bareev – I.Sokolov
Madrid 1994

White has the advantage since his pawn structure is more compact and his king is already centralised. He plans &d4 and &c5, winning either the b-pawn or the d-pawn. Resolute action is therefore demanded of Black.

29 ...   Ra6!

Redeploying his rook to a more active square.

30 Rb2

Keeping pawns on the queenside is the only way of playing to win. After 30 Rxb4 Rxa2 it would still be a theoretical draw even if White somehow won the d5-pawn after 31 exd5 exd5 etc..

30 ...   Ra4!

Completing the rook manoeuvre. On a4 it has both an aggressive and defensive function. It is especially important that 31 &d4 is ruled out because of 31...b3+! This is a good example of a rook being better placed at the side rather than behind a pawn.

31	♔d3	♔f6
32	♔c2	♖a3!

The white king has to be kept out of b3.

33 ♔b1?

White correctly frees the rook from the defence of a2, although his king is now inactive. However, he should have prefaced this move with the exchange 33 exd5 exd5, when after 34 ♔b1 Black will be forced into the unpleasant variation of the next note.

33 ...   dxe4!

If 33...♖a4 then 34 exd5 exd5 35 ♖d2 ♔e5 36 ♔b2 threatening 37 ♔b3 is uncomfortable for Black, so he rightly looks for counterplay on the kingside.

34 ♖xb4   e3?

But this is wrong. He should keep the tension on the kingside with 34...♔f5. If then 35 ♔b2? ♖f3 wins the f2-pawn. So the game could have ended 35 ♖b7 ♔f6 36 ♖b4 ♔f5 etc., with a draw.

35 f3?

White responds with a serious mistake. Perhaps time-trouble blighted the play hereabouts? In any case, Bareev should have played 35 fxe3 when after 35...♖xe3 36 a4 e5 the impulsive move 37 a5? achieves nothing because of 37...♖a3 38 ♖b5 ♔f5. However, 37 ♔a2! leaves Black in trouble, e.g. 37...♖c3 (pushing the pawn fails: 37...e4 38 a5 ♖e1 39 a6 e3 40 a7 e2 41 ♖b6+ ♔f5 42 a8♕ etc.) 38 a5 ♔f5 39 a6 ♖c7 40 ♖a4 ♖a7 41 ♔b3 etc. and White should win.

35 ...   e5

Black now has the initiative. His active king and central passed pawn outweigh the white outside passed pawn.

36	♖e4	h5
37	♔b2	♖d3
38	a4	g5
39	h3	

Here 39 a5 is given as equal by Ivan Sokolov in *Informator 60*. However, 39...♖d5 40 ♖xe3 ♖xa5 is a little uncomfortable for White because his king is so far away from the kingside, and if the king tries to approach the kingside with 41 ♔c3, then 41...♖a2 wins the h-pawn.

39	...	e2
40	a5	♖xf3
41	a6?	

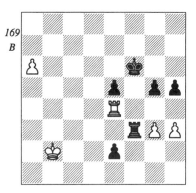

169
B

An instructive error.

Sokolov says that 41 ♖xe2 ♖xg3 42 a6 ♖d3 43 a7 ♖d8 44 ♔c3 draws. This seems correct, e.g. 44...♖a8 (44...♔f5 45 ♖b2 – threat 46 ♖b8 – ♖a8 46 ♖b7) 45 ♖a2 g4 46 hxg4 h4!? 47 ♔d3 ♔g5 48 ♔e4

♔xg4 49 ♔xe5 h3 50 ♔d5 ♔g3 51 ♔c6 h2 52 ♖xh2 ♔xh2 53 ♔b7.

41 ...   ♖d3!

White's 41st move leads to the forced loss of the a-pawn. Then, with his king stranded on the queenside, White's position becomes very difficult.

42 a7   ♖d8
43 ♖xe2   ♖a8
44 ♖f2+   ♔e6
45 g4   ♖xa7!

Avoiding the careless 45...hxg4? when after 46 hxg4 ♖xa7 47 ♖f5! ♖g7 48 ♔c3 ♔d5 49 ♔d3 White has an absolute blockade on the kingside comparable to that seen in the Gelfand-Kosashvili game on page 132. Instead Sokolov makes sure his rook stays active.

46 ♖f5

If 46 gxh5 then 46...♖h7 regains the pawn, and White no longer has the strong square on f5.

46 ...   ♖g7
47 ♔c3   h4

The presence of rook's pawns means that White cannot create a blockade, as will be seen.

48 ♔d3   ♖a7!
49 ♖xg5   ♔d5!

Precise play. Of course, White escapes with a draw after the continuation 49...♖a3+ 50 ♔e4 ♖xh3 (50...♖a4+ and 51...♔d5! is better) 51 ♖xe5+ etc.

50 ♖h5?

Imagine if the white g and h-pawns and the black h-pawn disappeared from the board. Then

White would draw if he were able to play ♖e8! (or rook to any other safe square behind the pawn). This would stop Black combining the advance of his e-pawn with driving the white king away from the queening square. Such a drawing method has already been described in our vital knowledge chapter: White would only have to play his rook to e8 and wait.

This means that in the game position White has to find a way to eliminate Black's h-pawn and then play ♖e8!, which would lead to a draw. However, if in capturing the h-pawn he misplaces his rook, then the vital move ♖e8 may be fatally delayed: Black would be able to use this time to establish a winning position before the rook reaches e8. This is what happens in the game, and White loses.

The best chance was to ignore Black's h-pawn and play 50 ♖g8! then 50...♖a3+ 51 ♔e2 ♔e4 52 g5!? or 52 ♖e8 may draw. For example, 52 ♖e8 ♖xh3 53 g5 ♖g3 (53...♔f5 54 g6 ♖g3 55 ♖h8 h3 56 g7 with a draw) 54 ♖h8! ♖xg5 55 ♖xh4+ and we have our theoretical draw. Or again, 52 ♖e8 ♔f4 53 g5 e4 54 g6 ♖a2+ 55 ♔e1 ♔e3 56 ♔f1 ♖f2+ 57 ♔g1 (57 ♔e1? ♖g2 threatens mate and ...♖xg6) 57...♖f6 58 ♖g8 ♔e2 59 g7 ♖g6+ 60 ♔h2 e3 61 ♔h1 ♖g5 62 ♔h2 ♖g3 63 ♔h1 ♖xh3+ 64 ♔g2 ♖g3+ 65 ♔h2 and it appears Black cannot win.

White has been outplayed, his situation is desperate, every Black move deserves an exclamation mark...yet still there was a good chance to draw after 50 ♖g8! Such is the drawing magic of rook and pawn endgames!

50 ...   **♖a3+**
51 ♔e2   **♔e4**

Bareev would be able to draw after 51...♖xh3 52 g5 by exchanging his g-pawn for the h-pawn, thereby achieving the theoretical draw described above at move 50.

52 ♖xh4?

Here 52 ♖h8! was the last hope for a draw, ignoring the h-pawn and heading straight for e8. The h-pawn proves poisoned.

52 ...   **♖a2+**
53 ♔d1   **♔d3**
54 ♔c1

The white king has to give way since if 54 ♔e1 e4 55 ♖h8 ♖a1+ 56 ♔f2 e3+ 57 ♔f3 ♖f1+ 58 ♔g2 e2 forces the pawn through. Now the rook on h4 is hopelessly out of play.

54 ...   **♖c2+!**
55 ♔b1

The white king has to move further away from the pawn as 55 ♔d1 ♖h2 56 ♔e1 e4 57 ♖h8 ♖h1+ 58 ♔f2 e3+ 59 ♔g2 e2 (Sokolov) queens the pawn.

Once again we notice that White is a tempo short to draw: if White's rook were on h8 rather than h4, he would draw with 55 ♔d1 ♖h2 56 ♔e1 e4 57 ♖e8 etc.

55 ...   **e4**
56 ♖h6   **♖g2**
57 ♖d6+   **♔e2**

The white rook has come to life, but a different theoretical endgame has arisen. Black has established a form of Lucena's position with the white king cut off from the black passed pawn. The rest is simple.

58 h4

If 58 ♔c2, then 58...e3 59 ♖f6 ♔e1+ 60 ♔d3 e2 (threat 61...♔d1) 61 ♔c2 ♖f2 62 g5!? ♔f1! and wins.

58 ...   **e3**
59 ♖f6

He has to prevent 59...♔f1 and 60...e2.

59 ...   **♔d2**
60 ♖d6+   **♔e1**
61 ♖f6   **♖f2**

and White resigned. Black promotes his e-pawn then picks off the white passed pawns.

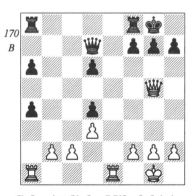

Schmittdiel – Mihalchisin
Bern 1994

Black is a pawn up, but he has two sets of doubled and isolated pawns.

20 ...   **♛b5!**

Offering an exchange of queens. If 21 ♕xb5 axb5, then the weakling on a4 suddenly becomes a potential passed pawn. White has no wish to strengthen Black's pawns and so avoids the exchange. However, in doing so he leaves his queenside pawns undefended. This allows Black to swap two sickly pawns for two of White's healthy ones, upon which his extra pawn becomes meaningful.

21 ♕f4   ♕xb2
22 ♖xa4   ♕xc2
23 ♕xd4   ♖fe8!

Black exploits White's weak back rank to activate his rooks with gain of time.

24 ♖ea1   ♖ab8!
25 h3   ♖b1+
26 ♔h2

If 26 ♖xb1 then 26...♕xb1+ 27 ♔h2 ♕b5 followed by ...♕c6, and Black has consolidated his extra pawn.

26 ...   ♖xa1
27 ♖xa1   ♕c6
28 ♕c4!?

A difficult choice. Mihalchisin thinks this is a blunder and recommends 28 ♖a5, when it is difficult for Black to make progress. However, White plays according to the principle that all rook endings are drawn, and it seems he was correct.

28 ...   ♕xc4
29 dxc4   ♖a8!

Now the rook is in its ideal position behind the passed pawn.

30 ♖d1

This is White's idea. He regains his pawn since 30...♖d8 31 ♖a1 ♖a8 32 ♖d1 draws. However, Black is able to activate his king and this, combined with the outside passed pawn, makes things difficult for White.

30 ...   a5
31 ♖xd6   ♔f8!

Mihalchisin analyses 31...a4 to a draw in *Informator 60*: 32 c5 a3 33 c6 and now 33...a2? 34 c7 is best avoided by Black. A possible finish would be 33...♔f8 34 c7 ♔e7 35 ♖a6! with a draw after 35...♖c8. The trick ♖a6! with the white pawn on c7 is a very important drawing device for White, as will be seen in what follows.

32 ♔g3?

A critical moment. White tries to bring his king into active play but it is all too late. Nevertheless, the drawing magic of rook and pawn endgames would have saved White if he had remembered that passed pawns should be pushed: **32 c5!** Now Mihalchisin claims that Black has a winning position after 32...♔e7 33 ♖d2? ♖c8! 34 ♖c2 (the white rook is forced to leave the d-file which allows the black king to cross to the queenside; of course 34 ♖a2 ♖xc5 defends a5) 34...♔e6 35 c6 ♔d6 36 ♖a2 ♖a8 37 ♖c2 ♔c7! The black king blocks the c-pawn and Black is ready to advance ....a4-a3. Then the white rook will be diverted from the defence of his passed pawn, and ....♔xc6 will win easily.

However, after **32...♔e7** White can play **33 ♖d5!** (rather than 33 ♖d2?). Then he should draw, e.g.

a) 33...♖c8 34 c6! attacking a5.

b) 33...♔e6 34 ♖d6+! ♔e5 35 f4+! (by sacrificing the f-pawn, White deflects the black king and allows the passed c-pawn to be activated) 35...♔xf4 36 c6 ♔e5 (36...a4 37 c7 a3? 38 ♖d8) 37 ♖d1 a4 (37...♖a7 38 ♖d7 ♖a6 39 ♖xf7 ♖xc6 40 ♖a7! – stopping ...♖a6 – 40...♖c5 41 ♖xg7 draws) 38 c7 ♖c8 39 ♖a1 ♖xc7 40 ♖xa4 and Black's extra kingside pawn doesn't give any realistic winning chances.

c) 33...♖d8 34 ♖e5+ ♔f6 (or 34...♔d7 35 c6+! draws at once) 35 f4 etc. and Black cannot progress.

d) 33...a4 34 c6 and now:

d1) 34...♖a7 35 ♖d3 a3 36 c7 ♖xc7 37 ♖xa3 draws.

d2) 34...a3 35 c7 a2 and now rather than 36 ♖a5? ♖xa5 37 c8♛ a1♛ White should play 36 ♖d1 and Black can do nothing to win.

In these variations it will be seen that White's rook successfully cut off the black king's approach to the queenside. Black wasn't able to force the white rook away from the d-file without either losing his a-pawn or being obliged to exchange it for the c-pawn. This meant that Black's king proved almost as passive as White's king when it came to influencing the play on the queenside.

White's move in the game proved too slow.

32 ...   a4
33 ♔f3

If 33 c5 a3 34 c6 a2 and White loses because he is a tempo down on variation d2 above, but now the a-pawn proves too strong.

33 ...   a3
34 ♖d1   ♔e7
35 ♔e3   a2
36 ♖a1   ♔d6
37 ♔d4   ♖a4!

With his rook immobile, White will be in zugzwang as soon as he runs out of kingside pawn moves.

38 f4

If 38 ♔c3 then 38...♔c5 39 ♔b3 ♖b4+! 40 ♔c3 (40 ♔xa2 ♖a4+ 41 ♔b2 ♖xa1 42 ♔xa1 ♔c4 and Black will capture White's kingside pawns after ...♔d3 etc.) 40...♖xc4+ 41 ♔b3 ♖b4+ 42 ♔c3 ♖a4 43 ♔b3 ♖a8 (intending to play ...♔d4) 44 ♔c3 ♖a3+ 45 ♔b2 ♔b4 and wins.

38 ...   h5
39 g4   h4
40 g5   g6

White resigned. It is zugzwang, and White will lose as in the note above.